SNORING AS A FINE ART
AND
TWELVE OTHER ESSAYS

SNORING AS A FINE ART
AND
TWELVE OTHER ESSAYS

By
Albert Jay Nock

Essay Index Reprint Series

 BOOKS FOR LIBRARIES PRESS
FREEPORT, NEW YORK

These Essays were selected
in memory of

Albert Jay Nock

by his friends
of many years

Ruth Robinson
Ellen Winsor
Rebecca Winsor Evans

INTERNATIONAL STANDARD BOOK NUMBER:
0-8369-2007-4

LIBRARY OF CONGRESS CATALOG CARD NUMBER:
77-121493

PRINTED IN THE UNITED STATES OF AMERICA

ACKNOWLEDGMENTS

Permission to reprint the essays herein has been graciously granted by the original copyright owners specified below. Since publication, however, the ownership of the several copyrights has been transferred to the author's son, Dr. Francis Jay Nock.

The American Mercury:

What the American Votes For. February 1933

The Atlantic Monthly:

If Only— August 1937
Sunday in Brussels. September 1938
Snoring As a Fine Art. November 1938
The Purpose of Biography. March 1940
Epstean's Law. October 1940
Utopia in Pennsylvania: The Amish. April 1941

The Bookman:

Bret Harte as a Parodist. May 1929

Harper's Magazine:

Alas! Poor Yorick! June 1929
The King's Jester: Modern Style. March 1928

Scribner's Magazine:

Henry George: Unorthodox American. November 1933
Life, Liberty, And— March 1935

The Sewanee Review:

Advertising and Liberal Literature. Winter 1918

CONTENTS

▼

INTRODUCTION

By Suzanne La Follette

A FRIEND who saw a great deal of Albert Jay Nock during his long sojourns in Belgium once said to me, "I don't know how he does it; but when you're with Albert Nock you find yourself coming out with things you didn't know you had it in you to say."

This effect of certain rich personalities on those privileged to associate with them is not easy to explain; more especially since not all rich personalities produce it. Perhaps it is brought about by a spiritual courtesy; a tolerant expectancy; possibly, more than anything else, by a willingness to help the truth along without encumbering it with themselves, to use an expression which Albert Nock was fond of quoting. Nock, for example, was temperamentally incapable of taking you down, when you mentioned a good idea that had just come to you, with, "Of course. That is exactly what I said in my last article." (In all the years I knew him, I never once heard him quote himself.) He tacitly granted your right to independent discovery and discussed your offering on its merits.

But why speculate on a quality so elusive as the gift of stimulating people to be better than they are? It is wiser merely to bear witness; as Edward Epstean did (that racy character and friend of the *Freeman* staff to whom "Epstean's Law" is playfully ascribed in these essays). When the *Freeman* was about to cease publication after four wonderful and financially unprofitable years, he remarked to Albert Nock:

"You've done a great deal for all those young people."

"I don't know that I've ever done anything for them except let them alone," said Nock.

"Yes, I understand," answered Epstean. "But if someone else had been letting them alone, it would have been a very different story."

Yet I don't think Albert Nock was primarily interested in people. He was much too fastidious; a true intellectual aristocrat. Indeed, there were even some who thought him an intellectual snob, and little did he care, for he was indifferent to gossip about himself and never gossiped about others. People *qua* people rather appalled him, and the ascendancy of mass man in modern society and the councils of government filled him with the horror that emerges from these essays. There frequently crept into his work after *Freeman* days more than a touch of his disdain for the cheapness and vulgarity of the life that followed World War One. I remember once suggesting—it was in the late twenties—that it was likely to antagonize those whom otherwise he might persuade. He said he thought I was probably right, but I think my lament left him essentially indifferent.

He was interested in ideas ("The idea," he once wrote, "is forever the fact"). He was interested in intelligent and civilized people. And he was above all interested in ability. The nearest he ever came to boasting was in his claim to instinctive recognition of ability. Character, he would say, eluded him; he could not judge it; but on ability no one could fool him.

He was not only interested in ability; he sought it out and encouraged it. He gave it a chance to develop by letting it alone in his own very special way. Not as a conscious service to society or his country or even to the beneficiary. It was, I suppose, the teacher's instinct in him; the instinct to serve truth. But he never tried to impose *his* truth on his pupil. Rather, he was concerned to put the pupil in the way to find truth for himself—as if he had revised the Biblical saying, "Ye shall know the truth, and the truth shall make you free," to read, "Ye shall be free in order that ye may know the truth." Nor was he looking for gratitude. "You don't try to repay the help that is given you," he would say. "You pass it along to others."

He passed along to "those young people" freedom to develop in their own way, to find their own truth. He himself had a gift for grasping the importance of truths so obvious that almost everyone overlooks them. One of these—the one that more than anything else made him a great editor—was that any organization is *people*, and that no organization can be better or other than the people who compose it. His interest as an editor was in the people who produced the magazine. I remember an impromptu talk he made to the staff one day at lunch, after the *Freeman* had been publishing six months. He had not worried about the quality of the magazine, he told us, for if the people engaged in an enterprise were happy and growing in their work, the enterprise was bound to reflect their spiritual state. He felt that the people connected with the *Freeman* were happy in their work, and growing in it; and so long as that was true the magazine could not be other than excellent.

The reader of this little book will find expressed in it again and again this awareness that organizations are *people*. As the *Freeman's* guiding spirit he put it to good service. He brought together a group of people whom he considered able, and ensured the health of the organization by the simple method of letting them alone.

I have dwelt at this length upon Albert Nock's relations with "those young people" of the *Freeman* because it seems to me that his editorship of that magazine which he made so remarkable is an index to the character and influence of a very remarkable man; a man who was a libertarian not only in theory but in practice, and who—*mirabile dictu*—wanted liberty for others as much as for himself; who clearly realized, indeed, that without liberty man is a slave no matter how many subsidies and services officious overlords may impose upon him.

Liberty was the touchstone by which he tested the quality of social life: the relations between man and man, man and society, man and the state. It is faith in liberty which inspires these essays (for whose preservation we owe a great debt to Mrs. Evans and the Misses Robinson and Winsor), as in fact it inspired everything he wrote. He rejected the Welfare State because he knew that the ministrations of its swarming bureaucracy interfere with the individual's pursuit of happiness—"Can any individual be happy when he is continually conscious of not being his own man?" And also because he knew that the arrogation to itself of the power to regulate the conduct of the citizen interferes with the legitimate functions of the state, which are two: "first freedom; second, justice." In other words, the state's business is to *let people alone*, and to coerce them only in the measure necessary to ensure their letting one another alone.

It was this passion for liberty—for letting people alone—which filled him with abhorrence of the ubiquitous Peeping Tom curiosity about personal lives. It is well expressed in the essay on "The Purpose of Biography," with its severe strictures on the vulgar sensationalism of much that is accepted today as serious biographical writing. And his own biographical essay on Henry George excellently illustrates his idea of biographical method; a method which rigorously excludes all personal data not relevant to the public character and history of the subject. No doubt if biographers conformed to his canon of admissible evidence the public appetite, and the market, for biography would decline. But there is equally no doubt that public taste and the quality of historical writing would benefit immeasurably.

I do not mean to give the impression that Albert Nock

was in any sense a propagandist or a fanatic. Were I to try, the range of interest, the mellowness and urbanity revealed in this book would amply disprove me. But I think I am not wrong in ascribing the lucidity of his thought and even of his style to his profound understanding of the meaning of freedom and the wealth of its implications.

So little was there of the propagandist in him that he never seemed much interested in the fate of his work. He once wrote me a remarkable letter of advice in which he expressed succinctly his idea of a writer's duty to himself: "Write what you want to write, as well as you can, and then forget it." He was not eager for fame; he had a greater ambition. He aspired to *excellence*, and well did he know how few and obscure, in these times, are its devotees. He wrote comparatively little, as a sensitive writer must in an age whose tastes and mores are the opposite of his own. But he wrote that little "as well as he could," and that was well indeed; so well that while there are still a few who love freedom, wisdom, excellence of thought and style, those few will be his readers. And they are the only readers he would want.

SNORING AS A FINE ART

And the Claims of General M. I. Kutusov As an Artist

I

WHAT COLOSSAL irony!" I said to myself as I closed Caulaincourt's memoirs of the Russian campaign of 1812. "It seems that Napoleon was utterly ruined and Napoleonic France was utterly destroyed, all by a man who actually did nothing about it but snore through staff meetings, write sprightly letters to Madame de Staël, read French novels, and hold his army back as tight as he could from aggressive military operations of any kind. What a distressing thought to carry to St. Helena!"

The rationale of the Russian campaign seems to have been a standing puzzle to historians on both sides. Some seventy years ago Count Tolstoy published a book called *War and Peace*, in which he undertook to show that both the Russian and the French historians were equally all wrong, and that the real rationale of the campaign was something quite different. Later historians, with the usual fine professional contempt for secular learning, paid little attention to Count Tolstoy's views, and, as far as I know, have never thought them worth discussing.

But now comes Caulaincourt's journal, which backs up Count Tolstoy's conclusions with astonishing particularity, and makes it pretty clear that the old Count was right. I was so struck by this that I got out my dog-eared copy of *War and Peace* and penciled cross-references between it and Caulaincourt's journal, with results which convinced me that in all essential respects the old man had a large edge on the historians. If any reader has curiosity enough to put the two books side by side and read from one to the other, as I did, I believe he will come away with the same opinion.

This Caulaincourt was Napoleon's right-hand man in the campaign. They saw it through together, and when at last Napoleon deserted the pitiful remnant of his soldiery and ran away to Paris, Caulaincourt went with him and loyally stuck by him to the last; he was about the only one who did. Throughout the campaign, Caulaincourt kept a full journal of each day's doings; it is one of the most fascinating books I ever read. This journal did not see daylight for a century; it was supposed to be lost. It was discovered, I believe by accident, five or six years ago; it was then published, and has lately been translated into English.

The one thing which perhaps has been most bothersome to historians, especially Russian historians, is that if the Russian commander had done everything that they all assume a good general should have done, he could have made a most spectacular military success. He did none of those things, however, though everyone expected them. The Tsar expected them; so did the court and all Russian officialdom, and the entire Russian staff; and so, above all, did the French. Nothing in Caulaincourt's whole story is more interesting than his naïve disclosure of French bewilderment at Kutusov's[1] actions.

Early in the campaign, when Kutusov took up an impregnable position at Maley-Yaroslavetz and then most unaccountably and unreasonably abandoned it overnight,

[1] Field Marshal Prince Mihail Ilarionovitch Kutusov-Smolensky (1745-1813); served under Suvorov, gaining a great military reputation; twice governor of Vilna; commanded the Russian forces against Napoleon at Austerlitz; commanded against the Turks, 1810-1811; commander in chief against Napoleon, 1812.—AUTHOR

Caulaincourt reports Napoleon's saying, "That devil Kutusov will never make a fight of it." Nor did he. On the great retreat from Moscow, he could have captured Napoleon, Murat, Davoût, Ney, anyone he liked, a dozen times over. He could have cut off the retreat, devastated the French army, slaughtered thousands, taken prisoners wholesale and raised the devil generally, all to the praise and glory of holy Russia. At the campaign's end, Napoleon walked straight into a nutcracker at the Berezina; he had Wittgenstein's army closing in on his right, Kutusov's own army on his left, and waiting for him in front, on both ends of the Berezina bridge, was Tchitchagov; but Kutusov did not close the nutcracker. Instead, he ordered Wittgenstein to slow up a little, slowed up his own march, and sent word to Tchitchagov to keep his eyes open and take it easy.

Nobody understood these tactics. After Maley-Yaroslavetz, Napoleon said to Caulaincourt, "I beat the Russians every time, but that does not get me anywhere." From then on, Caulaincourt reveals the amazement of the French at almost every step. Why abandon one good position after another? Why not follow up the advantage at Tarutino, Krasnoe, Vyazma? Why not cut off the retreat at this, that, or the other point? Why above all, since Tchitchagov had kept the French under close observation at the Berezina for thirty-six hours, did he not send out a stand of cannon and blow them to Jericho while they were crossing the river on their improvised bridges?

The Petersburg court and the official set were equally mystified, and also disgusted; no more so than the Tsar, who never liked Kutusov, and had repeatedly blistered him for his inaction. Kutusov's own staff had given him up as hopeless. They would meet, discuss aggressive strategy, urge attacks, plan battles, suggest forays, and all that sort of thing, while the old man's nose sent forth loud trumpeting sounds which betokened a complete lack of interest; and when at last they had it all out of their systems, he would wake up and mutter something to the effect that the supplies had not come up yet, or the soldiers' boots were worn out, or the troops did not know how to execute such complicated manœuvres; and that would be that.

So some historians put it that Kutusov was no better than an "old dowager," as Napoleon called him, an incompetent and crafty courtier, not worth his salt as a soldier. The trouble with that theory is that he had a gilt-edged record all the way down from Suvorov's time to his conclusive windup of the Turkish war in 1811, only a few months before Napoleon crossed the frontier. Others put it that he was a weak and dissolute old man, too far gone in his dotage to know what he was about; but that will hardly wash either, for, hang it all, he got results. When his lackadaisical campaign was over, Napoleon was finally and completely done in; done in for good and all—Waterloo was only a *coup de grâce*. Napoleonic France was also permanently done in; and when the *Grande Armée* straggled across the border there was not enough of it left to be worth counting.

What more could one ask? Even the Tsar had to bottle up his chagrin in face of the fact that, even if his old general's management had not been exactly what one would call stylish, it had nevertheless somehow turned the trick in the cheapest and most effective way.

II

Two things revealed by the composite Tolstoy-Caulaincourt narrative struck me with peculiar force. The first is that from the moment Moscow was captured and occupied Kutusov seems to have known exactly what Napoleon was going to do. Moreover, it is clear that he was the only one who did know. Caulaincourt shows beyond peradventure that through the whole month spent in Moscow Napoleon himself had not the faintest idea of what his own next move would be; nor, naturally, had anyone on the French side, and of course no one but Kutusov on the Russian side had any idea of it, especially in view of circumstances which I shall presently mention.

Something like this had happened once before. Kutusov commanded the Russian forces at Austerlitz; and there too he knew exactly what Napoleon was going to do. He warned the Russian and Austrian emperors that if they took the offensive, as they and the Austrian strategists were keen for doing, the battle would be a total loss because Napoleon was not going to do anything like what they were expecting, but something quite different. If his advice had been taken, it is anybody's guess what might have been the outcome. He was overruled, however, and the thing turned out precisely as he had said it would. He presided at the staff meeting held the evening before the attack, and throughout the two hours consumed by the Austrian general Weyrother in reading the disposition of the troops he was sound asleep and snoring manfully. In the battle next day he acted with great energy and ability, but he knew that no matter how the troops were disposed the battle would be lost by reason of contingencies which he, and no one else, foresaw.

After the occupation of Moscow, however, the case was different. Kutusov could not tell the Tsar or anyone else what he knew, because it was something so fantastically improbable that he would instantly have been deprived of his command, if not certified to an asylum as a hopeless lunatic. Napoleon was a good officer; he was supposed to be the best general in Europe. He had already conquered a large slice of Russia and had taken Moscow. After that, there were several courses equally open to him, any one of which a good officer might creditably choose. The course which he actually did choose, however, and which Kutusov apparently knew he would choose, was one that no kind of officer, even a shavetail lieutenant just out of West Point, would ever dream of taking.

Napoleon could have wintered in Moscow, where, as the French historians admit, he had six months' supplies available, despite the fire. He could have rested and refitted his army there for a week or so, and then pushed on to threaten Petersburg (which Alexander I thought he would do) and negotiated an advantageous peace. He could have moved over to Nizhni-Novgorod, or, if he wished to shorten up his communications, he could have fallen back on Smolensk or Vilna for the winter. The road into the rich southern provinces was open to him; so was practically any road anywhere, in fact, for Kutusov was encamped in front of Kaluga, offering him no obstruction, but merely lying low and waiting for the outcome which he had foreseen as inevitable, and on which he was confidently risking the whole fate of Russia. Again, if Napoleon had decided to retreat, he might have retreated through a region well furnished with supplies, by the road along which Kutusov subsequently pursued him; or, as one might better say, chaperoned him.

With all these choices before him, what Napoleon actually did was to remain idle in Moscow for a month; then march out, ill-prepared and at the very worst time of year, in a half-hearted search for the Russian army; and then, after the indecisive collisions at Maley-Yaroslavetz and Tarutino, which Kutusov did his best to avoid, he broke into a headlong stampede for the frontier by the worst route he could have chosen—the road by Mozhaisk towards Smolensk, which led through utterly devastated regions. Who could possibly have predicted anything like that from the greatest military genius of Europe? Yet, as I say, apparently Kutusov knew Napoleon would do just that, and knew it so well that with Tsar and court and his own staff all against him he staked the future, not only of Russia but of Europe, on his knowledge.

Kutusov seems to have been one of those peculiarly and

mysteriously gifted persons of whom one can say only, as we so often do say in our common speech, that they "had something." Such people appear in history all the way from Balaam the son of Beor down to contemporary examples which I shall presently cite; there are more of them, perhaps, than one would think. They "have something," but nobody knows what it is or how they got it; and investigation of it is always distinctly unrewarding. In the late J. A. Mitchell's story called *Amos Judd*—one of those sweet and unpretentious little narratives of the last century which I suppose no one nowadays could be hired to read—Deacon White says, "There's something between Amos and the Almighty that the rest of us ain't into"; and that is about as far as scientific inquiry into these matters has ever carried us, or probably ever will.

Yet the something is there. We can all cite instances of it in our most commonplace experience, without troubling to look up impressive historical examples. A friend who was wading through the Barchester series last winter remarked to me that it had an inordinate number of dull pages, "but the odd thing is that one doesn't skip them." Another friend not long ago asked me what makes Edward FitzGerald a great letter-writer. The answer is, of course, that nothing does; he simply isn't. Yet if you start reading his letters, trivial and actually uninteresting as they are, you keep on reading and rereading; and I do not believe Oxford's whole Faculty of Literature, in council assembled, could account for your doing it in terms which would boil down to anything more scientifically respectable than "because you do." What makes Madame Mertens, contralto at the Brussels opera, a great artist? Again, nothing; she isn't; not voice, not method, beauty, grace of movement, sex attraction, dramatic power, nor any combination of them. Like Trollope and FitzGerald, she simply has something; some fascinating endowment which keeps your recollection of her fresh and clear long after the memory of this-or-that really great artist has faded.

The peculiar something which Kutusov had, the "something between Amos and the Almighty" which made him so confidently aware that the unlikeliest thing in the world was the thing which was going to happen, seems to be entirely dissociated from intellect and personal will. Count Tolstoy says that young Prince Bolkonsky went away from an interview with Kutusov feeling greatly reassured about the old general's conduct of the campaign, because "he will put nothing of himself into it. He will contrive nothing, will undertake nothing. . . . He knows that there is something stronger and more important than his will; that is, the inevitable march of events; and he can see them and grasp their significance; and seeing their significance, he can abstain from meddling, from following his own will and aiming at something else."

The whole passage in *War and Peace* which describes this interview is worth a great deal of close meditation; it is the fifteenth and sixteenth chapters of Part X.

I shall return to this aspect of the matter in a moment. Before doing so I wish to remark that the gift (I call it a gift only for convenience, to save words) which we are discussing is not only dissociated from intellect, but also from conventional morals. Certain Old Testament characters who unquestionably had it, and on occasion let it put itself to good use, were nevertheless what by our conventional ethical standards we would call pretty tough citizens; our old friend Balaam, for instance, and Elisha. It has been said, and I believe it is accepted in some quarters—of course there is no knowing—that Joan of Arc was not in all respects a model of sound peasant character; but granting it be so, she still most conspicuously "had the goods."

Kutusov himself, like Lieutenant-General Bangs in Kipling's amusing ballad, had the reputation of being "a most immoral man." At sixty-three, very big, very fat, with one eye blinded and his face scarred by a bullet in one of Suvorov's wars, he seems somehow to have kept his attractiveness to the ladies, for his friendships with them—some of high degree, some not so high—were many and close. Even during his fourteen months' stay in Bucharest while he was starving out the Turks, he passed his enforced idleness in dalliance with a handsome and spirited Wallachian gal; rumors whereof got back to Petersburg, to the great scandal and discomposure of Alexander's court, for which he seems to have cared not a button. "The Spirit breathes where it will," said the *Santissimo Salvatore;* and oftentimes the breath of its most intimate inspiration blows upon persons whom we, in our modesty, would at once put down as morally disqualified.

The other striking impression which I got from the Caulaincourt-Tolstoy narrative was of Kutusov's attitude of complete quiescence towards the something which he had. Not only is that something, as I said, dissociated from intellect, but also if the intellect be applied to it in any attempt at rationalization, however cautious and tentative, it refuses to turn its game for you and leaves you in the lurch.

The case of the poet Wordsworth, for example, strongly suggests that this is so. Wordsworth unquestionably had something; and when he was content to leave that something in full charge of his poetical operations—when he resolutely bottled up the conscious and intellectual Wordsworth, and corked it down—he was a truly great poet. When he summoned up the conscious Wordsworth, however, and put it in charge, as unfortunately he too often did, the conscious Wordsworth was such a dreadful old foo-foo that the poetry churned out under its direction was simply appalling.

Kutusov seems to have done everything he could to keep his consciousness from playing upon the sequence of events which he alone knew was going to take place. In the chapters I have referred to (and I repeat, they are a great study)

Count Tolstoy says, "All Denisov had said was practical and sensible; what the general was saying was even more practical and sensible; but apparently Kutusov despised both knowledge and intellect, and was aware of something else which would settle things—something different, quite apart from intellect and knowledge." In view of this, he took every means to keep himself as nearly as possible in a state of complete selflessness. He attended to routine, watching everything, putting everything in its place, holding everything up to the mark; but beyond that he kept his mind as far off the actual course of the campaign as he could. He read French novels, corresponded with his lady-friends, meditated on all sorts of non-military matters; and, most effective and rewarding of all conceivable relaxations, he snored. Like nearly all old persons, he dropped off to sleep easily, almost at will; and being big and fat, he snored; and when a person is snoring he is about as inaccessible and unsuggestible and selfless as a living human being can become.

I once had an acquaintance whom I shall call Smith, for that is not his name; he is still alive and flourishing, I believe, and would presumably boggle at this kind of publicity. It was he who really completed my understanding of Kutusov's elaborately purposeful quiescence; not consciously, however, because, as I found out later, he had never even heard of Kutusov. Smith's career was unusual. He had great intelligence, ability, energy, determination, and in his earlier years he had thrown the whole sum of these into various enterprises, all of which went wrong. He wanted money, quite disinterestedly too, for he had some highly commendable semi-public purposes in view; but money ran like a scared dog whenever it saw him coming. Rather late in middle life (this is his own account of it) he discovered that he "had something," or that something had him; something, as Tolstoy says, quite apart from intellect and knowledge, which—provided he kept his conscious self in complete abeyance towards it—would really settle things. After that, everything he touched went right. I do not know how his affairs came out in the long run, this being some time ago, but at the period I speak of he appeared to be raking in money with both hands.

Smith told me most extraordinary stories of his prescience concerning the course of certain business operations; and since, like Kutusov, he had the goods to show for it, there seems no reasonable doubt that the stories were true. One which I remember particularly, since it brought Kutusov to my mind at once, was that he had just come from an important conference where the one thing most unlikely to happen had happened, precisely as he knew it would. "I was so sure of it," he said, "that when I went in I merely took my seat, said nothing, kept my mind as much as possible off the discussion, and waited for things to turn out as I expected; and so they did. If I had told anybody they would turn out that way, I should have been laughed at, but they did."

What most interested me about Smith was this attitude of studied quiescence. He had somehow, quite independently and off his own bat, formed the idea that the effort to do any examining or analyzing or rationalizing would be ruinous. I never saw a man who had such a nervous horror and hatred of "psychical research," or any kind of experimentation with spiritism, clairvoyance, telepathy, and the like. Rather to my surprise, since I did not suspect him of knowing our American classics, he cited Mr. Jefferson's remark about the virtue of resting one's head contentedly on the pillow of ignorance which the Creator has made so soft for us because He knew we should have so much use for it. Smith's philosophical position, as I understood it, was that of an intensively ignorant and incurious pragmatism. There the thing is, and it works; that is all one knows, and for all practical purposes it is all one needs to know. The attempt to discover anything about what it is, or how or why it works, is unfruitful, and apparently will always be so; and it seems also to be invariably damaging. Besides, Smith asked pointedly, if you should conceivably get anywhere with this sort of research, or even supposing you got as far as you can possibly imagine yourself getting, what good would it do?

Association with Smith kept continually bringing to my mind the profound saying of Joubert, that "it is not hard to know God, provided you do not trouble yourself to define Him." Smith carried his diffidence even to the point of having a great dread of verbal symbols; he never used them. They might be all right, he said, if it were clearly understood that they had no definite significance, but it was hard to keep up that clear understanding even with oneself, because, as Goethe says, man never knows how anthropomorphic he is; therefore one had best steer clear of them. The old prophet spoke of "the word which the Lord hath put in my mouth"; Socrates and Marcus Aurelius spoke of "the intimations of the dæmon." Such symbols might be all well enough, Smith said, as long as one were sure they were not being made to mean something; but it is hard to be always sure of that, and anyway they are unnecessary, so why not give them a wide berth? Organized Christianity, for example, had put a good many such symbols into currency and had attached definite meanings to them, or tried to, and see what a terrific lot of damage it has done!

With one exception, I am sure that Smith is the only man who ever discussed this subject with me. The other one was a retired gambler; it is really quite embarrassing that both my prize exhibits should be such as the righteous would at once frown upon as men of sin, for Smith also was no great shakes at either conventional piety or conventional morals. The ex-gambler told me he perfectly understood what I was driving at. Quite often in his career of skinning the unwary, he said—not always, but fairly often—he had sat into a game with a clear presentiment of how it would turn out.

If he knew he would lose, he lost in spite of all the skill and brainwork he could put into the effort to beat his presentiment; but he had discovered that if he were due to win he could do so only if he resolutely kept all brainwork off the game and played it out mechanically, simply "going along." If he did that, he said, he never failed to win.

III

And now I ask myself why I have burdened the printing press with this rather rambling and inconsequent recital. I hardly know. What I have written is not at all the kind of essay for which editors believe our "reading public," whatever that is, to be always thirsting. As the good and great John Bright said of Artemus Ward's lecture, "its information is meagre, and presented in a desultory, disconnected manner." As I rake over the débris of my thoughts, the only semblance of a purpose I can discover is to suggest that possibly, under certain circumstances, snoring should be regarded as a fine art and respected accordingly. If this be admitted, I might suggest further that our civilization does not so regard it, as it should, and gives the practice no encouragement, but rather the contrary.

Consequently one might with reason think that there is too little snoring done—snoring with a purpose to guide it, snoring deliberately directed towards a salutary end which is otherwise unattainable—and that our society would doubtless be better off if the value of the practice were more fully recognized. In our public affairs, for instance, I have of late been much struck by the number of persons who professedly had something. The starry-eyed energumens of the New Deal were perhaps the most conspicuous examples; each and all, they were quite sure they had something. They had a clear premonition of the More Abundant Life into which we were all immediately to enter by the way of a Planned Economy. It now seems, however, that the New Deal is rapidly sinking in the same Slough of Despond which closed over poor Mr. Hoover's head, and that the More Abundant Life is, if anything, a little more remote than ever before.

I do not disparage their premonition or question it; I simply suggest that the More Abundant Life might now be appreciably nearer if they had put enough confidence in their premonition to do a great deal less thinking, planning, legislating, organizing, and a great deal—oh yes, a very great deal —more snoring.

"Counselors and counselors!" said Kutusov to Prince Bolkonsky. "If we had listened to all of them, we should be in Turkey now. We should not have made peace, and the war would never have been over. . . . Kamensky would have come to grief there if he hadn't died. He went storming fortresses with thirty thousand men. It's easy enough to take fortresses, but it's hard to finish off a campaign successfully. Storms and attacks are not what's wanted, but *time* and *patience*. Kamensky sent his soldiers to attack Rustchuk, but I trusted to them alone—time and patience—and I took more fortresses than Kamensky, and I made the Turks eat horseflesh."

He shook his head. "And the French shall, too. Take my word for it," cried Kutusov, growing warmer, and slapping himself on the chest, "I'll make them eat horseflesh!"

What in any case it all boils down to, I suppose, is the rather trite fact that merely "to have something" is by no means enough. If one is sure one has something, the next thing is to know what to do about it; and in most circumstances—in more, at any rate, than is commonly supposed— snoring is a sovereign procedure. It is presumable that many persons who have something, and know they have it, lose out on it by a futile effort to coördinate "the intimations of the dæmon" with suggestions of desire, curiosities of intellect, impulses of will. Thus they come to disbelieve in the something which they actually have, and to regard it as mere fantasy; and from this most unfortunate disability a resolute devotion to snoring would have saved them.

But I did not intend to moralize, knowing myself to be uncommonly puny at that sort of thing; so, in fear of being led further, I shall end my prosaic disquisition here.

LIFE, LIBERTY, AND . . .

For almost a full century before the Revolution of 1776 the classic enumeration of human rights was "life, liberty, and property." The American Whigs took over this formula from the English Whigs, who had constructed it out of the theories of their seventeenth-century political thinkers, notably John Locke. It appears in the Declaration of Rights, which was written by John Dickinson and set forth by the Stamp Act Congress. In drafting the Constitution of Massachusetts in 1779 Samuel and John Adams used the same formula. But when the Declaration of Independence was drafted Mr. Jefferson wrote "life, liberty, and the pursuit of happiness," and although his colleagues on the committee, Franklin, Livingston, Sherman, and Adams, were pretty well tinctured with Whig philosophy, they let the alteration stand.

It was a revolutionary change. "The pursuit of happiness" is of course an inclusive term. It covers property rights, because obviously if a person's property is molested, his pursuit of happiness is interfered with. But there are many interferences which are not aimed at specific property rights; and in so wording the Declaration as to cover all these interferences, Mr. Jefferson immensely broadened the scope of political theory—he broadened the idea of what government is for. The British and American Whigs thought the sociological concern of government stopped with abstract property rights. Mr. Jefferson thought it went further; he thought that government ought to concern itself with the larger and inclusive right to pursue happiness.

16

II

This clause of the Declaration has been a good deal in my mind lately because for the best part of a year I have been moving about in several countries, and have noticed that hardly anybody in any of them seemed happy. I do not say that the people I saw were sullen or gloomy, or that they no longer occupied themselves in their usual ways. What struck me was, simply, that the general level of happiness was not so high as I had been accustomed to see it some years ago. The people did not act like free people. They seemed under a shadow, enervated, *sat upon*. They showed little of the spontaneity of spirit which is a sure mark of happiness; even in their amusements they behaved like people who have something on their minds. Moreover, this decline of spirit apparently had little to do with "prosperity" or the lack of it. For all I could see, the prosperous were as dispirited as the unprosperous, and the well-to-do seemed not much, if any, happier than the poor.

But the interesting thing about this moral enervation was that so much of it, practically all of it, was attributable to nothing else but state action. Any thoughtful observer could not help seeing that it arose chiefly out of a long series of positive interferences with the individual's right to pursue happiness. Whether or not these interventions were justifiable on other grounds, it was clear that if the state really had any concern with the individual's pursuit of happiness, it had made a most dreadful mess of its responsibility. I noticed with interest, too, that all the countries I visited had some sort of political structure that could be called republican. That is to say, their sovereignty nominally resided in the people, and the people nominally created their governments. This brought to my mind Paine's saying that "when we suffer or are exposed to the same miseries *by* a government which we might expect in a country *without* government, our calamity is heightened by the reflection that we furnish the means whereby we suffer." As an exercise of the scientific imagination, I tried to make a fair conjecture at the question whether the aggregate of these peoples' happiness was appreciably greater under the governments they had than it would be if they had no government at all. I could not make out that it was. I am not prepared with any elaborate defence of my estimate, but I think I could at least set up a pretty good case for the proposition that they were not nearly so happy as they would be if their governments had been considerably less paternalistic.

I am very far from suggesting that these governments deliberately set out to make their peoples unhappy. The question of motive need not come in at all. In fact, we may admit that by every one of its interventions the state intended to raise the general level of happiness, and actually thought it would do so. The only thing we need observe is that quite evidently it had not done so, and that if it had acted differently it might have succeeded better. By consequence, if it were acting differently now, the prospect for an increase in these peoples' happiness hereafter might be brighter than it is.

How, then, should the state act? What is the utmost that the state can do to raise the general level of happiness? Mr. Jefferson's answer to this question can be put in few words —that it should mind its own business. But what is its business? In Mr. Jefferson's view its business is to protect the individual from the aggressions and trespasses of his neighbors, and beyond this, to leave him strictly alone. The state's whole duty is, first, to abstain entirely from any positive regulation of the individual's conduct; and, second, to make justice easily and costlessly accessible to every applicant. In its relations with the individual, the code of state action should be purely negative, more negative by 20 per cent than the Ten Commandments. Its legitimate concern is with but two matters: first, freedom; second, justice.

III

This was Mr. Jefferson's notion of the state's part in bringing about an ideal social order. All his life was devoted to the doctrine that the state should never venture into the sphere of positive regulation. Its only intervention upon the individual should be the negative one of forbidding the exercise of rights in any way that interferes with the free exercise of the rights of others. According to this idea, one could see that the unhappiness and enervation which I was everywhere observing as due to state action were due to state action entirely outside the state's proper sphere. They were due to the state's not minding its own business but making a series of progressive encroachments on the individual's business. They were due to the state's repeated excursions out of the realm of negative coercion into the realm of positive coercion.

The frequency, variety, and extent of these excursions as disclosed by the last twenty years of European history are almost beyond belief. Tracing them in detail would be impracticable here, and is probably unnecessary. Any one acquainted with European conditions twenty years ago will be pretty well able to judge by how much the margin of existence, which the individual is free to dispose of for himself, has been reduced. Here or there in Europe the state now undertakes to tell the individual what he may buy and sell; it limits his freedom of movement; it tells him what sort of quarters he may occupy; what he may manufacture; what he may eat; what the discipline of his family shall be; what he shall read; what his modes of entertainment shall be. It "man-

ages" his currency, "manages" the worth of his labor, his
sales-prices and buying-prices, his credit, his banking-
facilities, and so on with an almost limitless particularity; and
it keeps an enormous, highly articulated bureaucracy standing over him to see that its orders are carried out.

This, too, when one considers only the positive coercions
that the state applies directly to the individual. When one
considers also those that it applies indirectly, one sees that
the individual's margin of free existence has well-nigh disappeared bodily. These coercions take place when the state in-
vades fields of endeavor that were formerly occupied by
private enterprise, and either competes with private enterprise or supplants it. In the countries that I visited, the state
now appears variously as railway-operator, ship-operator,
ship-builder, house-builder, clothier, shoemaker, gunmaker,
wholesale and retail tobacconist, match-seller, banker and
money-lender, news-purveyor, radio-broadcaster, market-
operator, aviation-enterpriser, letter-carrier, parcel-carrier,
telegraphist, telephonist, pawnbroker. The state has also invaded the field of eleemosynary effort, or what is called, I
believe, "social service." Thus the state now appears as grand
almoner, giving away immense largesse in the form of doles
or wage-supplements. It also appears as employer-at-large,
improvising work for those who have none. It also appears
as educator-in-chief, chief sanitary inspector, chief arbitra-
tor, chief druggist and chemist, chief agriculturalist, and in
many like rôles; in one country I noticed that the state had
even undertaken a loose monopoly of the dissemination of
culture! I can think of only one line of human activity—religion—in which state meddling has of late years tended rather
to decrease than to increase. Formerly the state was a considerable purveyor of religious opportunity, but now it does
very little actively in that way, its subsidies being mostly
confined to tax-exemption, as in the United States.

IV

By way of consequence, two things are noticeable. The first one is that whatever the state has accomplished outside its own proper field has been done poorly and expensively. This is an old story, and I shall not dwell upon it. No complaint is more common, and none better founded, than the complaint against officialism's inefficiency and extravagance. Every informed person who is at the same time disinterested is aware—often by harassing experience—that as compared with the administration of private enterprise, bureaucratic administration is notoriously and flagrantly slow, costly, inefficient, improvident, unadaptive, unintelligent, and that it tends directly to become corrupt. The reasons why this is so, and must be so, have often been set forth—the classic document in the case is Herbert Spencer's essay called *The New Toryism*—so I shall not go over them afresh, but merely cite one sample comparison which I was able to make, not in Europe, but here in America, and only the other day. I choose it merely for its vividness, since it concerns the one state enterprise which at present is considered the most laudable, most necessary, and most highly humanitarian.

About a week ago, I had by sheer accident an "inside" chance to compare American state enterprise with private enterprise in the matter of relief for certain enormous batches of destitute vagrants. The contrast was most impressive. If the co-operation of private enterprise had not stayed steadily on the spot to read the Riot Act to state enterprise, to show it which way to go and how to start, where to get off and how to stop when it got there, and in a general way hold its hand from beginning to end, those vagrants would have stood the best chance in the world not only of starving but of freezing, for a sudden spell of very bitter weather had just come on.

The clear consenting testimony of all political history certifies this incident as a standard specimen of state efficiency. The post office is often cited as an example of a state commercial monopoly that is well and cheaply administered. It is nothing of the kind. The post office merely sorts mail and distributes it. Private enterprise transports it; and as John Wanamaker said when he was Postmaster General, private enterprise would be only too glad to take over everything that the post office now does, do it much better and for much less money, and make an attractive profit out of it at that.

The second noticeable consequence of the state's activity in everybody's business but its own is that its own business is monstrously neglected. According to our official formula expressed in the Declaration, as I have said, the state's business is, first, with freedom; second, with justice. In the countries I visited, freedom and justice were in a very dilapidated condition; and the striking thing was that the state not only showed complete indifference to their breakdown, but appeared to be doing everything it could to break them down still further. As James Madison wrote in a letter to Mr. Jefferson in 1794, the state was busily "turning every contingency into a resource for accumulating force in the government," with a most callous disregard, not only of freedom and justice, but of common honesty. Every few days brought out some new and arbitrary confiscation of individual rights. Labor was progressively confiscated, capital was progressively confiscated, even speech and opinion were progressively confiscated; and naturally, in the course of this procedure anything like freedom and justice was ignored.

In short, I thought the people might fairly be said to be living for the state. The state's fiscal exactions, necessary to support its incursions into everybody's business but its own, were so great that their payment represented the confiscation of an unconscionable amount of the individual's labor and capital. Its positive regulations and coercions were so many, so inquisitorial, and their points of incidence upon the individual were so various, as to confiscate an unconscionable amount of his time and attention. Its enormously advantaged presence in so many fields of enterprise that are properly free and competitive confiscated an unconscionable share of his initiative and interest. It seemed to me that whichever way the individual turned, the state was promptly on hand to meet him with some form of positive coercion; at every step he was met by a regulation, an exaction, or a menace. Not daily but hourly, in the course of my travels, there occurred to me Mr. Henry L. Mencken's blunt characterization of the state as "the common enemy of all honest, industrious, and decent men."

So indeed it seemed. Putting the case in plain language, the individual was living in a condition of servitude to the state. The fact that he "furnished the means by which he suffered" —that he was a member of a nominally sovereign body— made his condition none the less one of servitude. Slavery is slavery whether it be voluntary or involuntary, nor is its character at all altered by the nature of the agency that exercises it. A man is in slavery when all his rights lie at the arbitrary discretion of some agency other than himself; when his life, liberty, property, and the whole direction of his activities are liable to arbitrary and irresponsible confiscation at any time—and this appeared to be the exact relation that I saw obtaining between the individual and the state.

V

This relation corresponds to a political theory precisely opposite to the one set forth in the Declaration. It is not a new theory; it is merely "cauld kail made het again," as the Scots say—it is the old doctrine of absolutism in a new mode or form. The theory behind the Declaration is that the state exists for the good of the individual, and that the individual has certain rights which are not derived from the state, but which belong to him in virtue of his humanity. He was born with them, and they are "unalienable." No power may infringe on them, least of all the state. The language of the Declaration is most explicit on this point. It is *to secure these rights*, Mr. Jefferson wrote, that governments are instituted among men. That is what government is for. The state may not invade these rights or abridge them; all it may do is to protect them, and that is the purpose of its existence.

The new absolutist theory of politics is exactly the opposite of this. The individual exists for the good of the state. He has no natural rights, but only such rights as the state provisionally grants him; the state may suspend them, modify them, or take them away at its own pleasure. Mussolini sums up this doctrine very handsomely in a single phrase, "Everything for the state; nothing outside the state; nothing against the state," and this is only an extension to the logical limit of the doctrine set forth in England by Carlyle, Professor Huxley, Matthew Arnold, and many others in the last century.

This idea, the absolutist idea of the state, seems to be very generally prevalent at the moment. The great majority of social philosophers and publicists treat it as matter-of-course; not only in Europe, where some form of theoretical absolutism has always been more or less in vogue, but also in America, where the idea of government, as expressed officially in the Declaration, runs all the other way. Since my return here I cannot help noticing that the rank and file of Americans seem to be extremely well reconciled to the idea of an absolute state, for the most part on pragmatic or "practical" grounds; that is to say, having found the frying-pan of a misnamed and fraudulent "rugged individualism" too hot for comfort, they are willing to take a chance on the fire. If only one be tactful enough not to name the hated names of Socialism, Bolshevism, Communism, Fascism, Marxism, Hitlerism, or what not, one finds no particular objection to the single essential doctrine that underlies all these systems alike —the doctrine of an absolute state. Let one abstain from the coarse word *slavery* and one discovers that in the view of many Americans—I think probably most of them—an actual slave-status is something that is really not much to be dreaded, but rather perhaps to be welcomed, at least provisionally. Such is the power of words.

The absolutist doctrine seems to assume that the state is a kind of organism, something that has an objective existence apart from the mere aggregation of individuals who make it up. Mussolini speaks of the state much as certain hierophants speak of the Church—as though if all its citizens died off overnight, the state would go on existing as before. So in the last generation Carlyle said that the state should be "the vital articulation of many individuals into a new collective individual"; and one hears the same sort of thing continually from the neo-absolutists of the present day.

No doubt this conception of the state has poetic truth, and to that extent there is a great deal in it. But in its practical relations with the individual, the state acts as though the idea also had scientific truth, which it manifestly has not. Merely reducing the matter to its lowest terms, as I did a moment ago, shows that it has not. Suppose every German died tonight, would the Hitlerian absolute state exist tomorrow in any but a strictly poetic sense? Clearly not.

Again, the absolutist rejection of the idea of natural rights lands one straight in the midst of the logical tangle that so baffled Herbert Spencer. If the individual has no rights but those that the state gives him, and yet if, according to republican theory, sovereignty resides in the people, we see a strange sort of sequence. Here we have a sovereign aggregation of individuals, none of whom has any rights of any kind. They create a government, which creates rights and then confers them on the individuals who created it. The plain man's wits do not hold out through this sequence, nor yet did Spencer's. "Surely," he says, "among metaphysical phantoms the most shadowy is this which supposes a thing to be obtained by creating an agent, which creates the thing, and then confers the thing on its own creator!"

But I do not intend to discuss these doctrines further; least of all do I intend to follow them into the shadowy realms of metaphysics. The thing that I am interested in for the moment is the pursuit of happiness. The question I wish to raise is whether it is possible for human beings to be happy under a régime of absolutism. By happiness I mean happiness. I do not mean the exhilaration arising from a degree of physical well-being, or the exaltation that comes from a brisk run of money-getting or money-spending, or the titillations and distractions brought on by the appeal to raw sensation, or the fanatical quasi-religious fervor that arises from participation in some mass-enterprise—as in Russia and Germany, at the moment. I refer to a stable condition of mind and spirit quite above anything of that kind; a condition so easily recognized and so well understood that I do not need to waste space on trying to define it.

Mr. Pickwick's acquaintance, Mr. Jack Hopkins, the young surgeon, thought a surgical operation was successful if it was skilfully done. Mr. Pickwick, on the other hand, thought it was successful if the patient got well. While in Europe I read a good many essays and speeches about public affairs, and they impressed me as having been written mostly from Mr. Jack Hopkins's point of view. Their burden was that the state's progressive confiscations, exactions and positive coercions, its progressive dragooning of the individual under bureaucratic management, were infallibly going to usher in a new Era of Plenty. If the state only kept on enlarging the scope of officialism, only kept on increasing its encroachments upon the individual's available margin of existence, it would round out an excellent social order and put it on a permanent footing.

Well, possibly. I have no inclination to dispute it, since even if the state were sure to do all this, I still have a previous question to raise. Like Mr. Pickwick, I am interested to know what the individual is going to be like when it is done. Let us make an extreme hypothesis. Let us suppose that instead of being slow, extravagant, inefficient, wasteful, unadaptive, stupid, and at least by tendency corrupt, the state changes its character entirely and becomes infinitely wise, good, disinterested, efficient, so that any one may run to it with any little two-penny problem and have it solved for him at once in the wisest and best way possible. Suppose the state close-herds the individual so far as to forestall every conceivable consequence of his own bad judgment, weakness, incompetence; suppose it confiscates all his energy and resources and employs them much more advantageously all round than he can employ them if left to himself. My question still remains—what sort of person is the individual likely to become under those circumstances?

I raise this question only because no one else seems ever to think of raising it, and it strikes me as worth raising. In all I have heard or read, in public or private, during the last four years, it has never once come up. I do not pretend to answer it. I raise it merely in the hope of starting the idea in the minds of others, for them to think about and answer for themselves, if they think it worth while to do so.

Can any individual be happy when he is continually conscious of not being his own man? Can the pursuit of happiness be satisfactorily carried on when its object is prescribed and its course charted by an agency other than oneself? In short, is happiness compatible with a condition of servitude, whether the voluntary servitude of the "yes-man" or the involuntary servitude of the conscript? How far is happiness conditioned by character, by keeping the integrity of one's personality inviolate, by the cultivation of self-respect, dignity, independent judgment, a sense of justice; and how far is all this compatible with membership in a conscript society? This is what I should like to hear discussed, for one hears nothing of it. If we might have this topic thoroughly threshed out for us in public now and again, I for one would not ask for another word about "a planned economy" and similar matters for a long time.

Crossing to America after the experiences I have mentioned, I read for the third time Mr. Aldous Huxley's *Brave New World*. Soon after arriving I read the extraordinary production called *Karl and the Twentieth Century*. I cannot recommend these books for purposes of entertainment; they are neither light nor particularly cheerful. One thing they do, however, and they do it exceedingly well. They throw a strong light, a very strong light indeed, upon what was probably in Mr. Jefferson's mind when he revised the classic enumeration of man's natural rights, and made it read, "life, liberty, and the pursuit of happiness." What I have seen since I landed has made me think it is high time for Americans to wake up to what the state is doing, and ask themselves a few plain questions about it. There are plenty of examples to show what a conscript society is like—well, do they want to live in one? There are plenty of examples to show what sort of people a conscript society breeds—is that the sort of people they want to be? Do they like the idea of a slave-status with a coercive and militant state as their owner? If they do, I should say they are getting what they want about as fast as is reasonably possible; and if they do not, my impression is that they had better not lose much time about being heard from.

UTOPIA IN PENNSYLVANIA:
THE AMISH

I

A LONG TIME ago, "when I was still a prince in Arcadia," I became interested in the language and literature of the Pennsylvania Germans. I had been rather astonished—I don't know why—at discovering accidentally that they had not only a literature of their own, but a good one, and that a thriving organization called the Pennsylvania German Society was busy fostering and preserving it. This was a pleasant surprise; and at odd times during two or three years I dipped at random into this literature, thus finally getting a fair-to-middling acquaintance with it, especially with its religious and pastoral poetry, the side by which it is seen in perhaps its most amiable and attractive aspect.

By origin, the Pennsylvania Germans spoke the dialect of the Pfalz; but in the course of a couple of centuries a good many English words have crept into their vocabulary to make everlasting sorrow and vexation for the outsider. A macaronic speech is easy enough to read when printed, but hardest of all (for me, at least) to understand when spoken. The Italian which one hears down Greenwich Village way in New York, for instance, is very difficult on this account, even when it is otherwise pretty good Italian. The Pfälzer dialect is not troublesome if you take it straight, but by the time you have shifted gears to accommodate two or three English words in the course of a long sentence, your interlocutor is away out of sight down the homestretch, leaving you in an exhausted and ignorant state; especially since the English words come out so heavily coated with a foreign inflection that it takes a minute or so to penetrate their disguise and recognize them. In dealing with the printed word, however, one escapes these tribulations. Here, for example, is the first stanza of a poem from Harbaugh's *Harfe*. Read it aloud at ordinary conversational speed to someone who knows German well, and see what he makes of it; then let him look at it as printed, and see whát he makes of that:

> *Heit is 's 'xäctly zwansig Johr,*
> *Dass ich bin owwe naus;*
> *Nau bin ich widder lewig z'rick*
> *Un schteh am Schulhaus an d'r Krick,*
> *Juscht neekscht an's Dady's Haus.*

The second verse is still more distressing. Here you have a colloquial English verb—slang, to the purist—handsomely tailored up with a good German prefix; and you have also an exact German rendering of an English idiomatic expression. These are heartbreakers; to the ear they carry nothing but grief and woe, yet see how familiar and domestic is their look in print:

> *Ich bin in hunnert Heiser g'west,*
> *Vun Märbelstee' un Brick,*
> *Un alles was sie hen, die Leit,*
> *Dhet ich verschwappe eenig Zeit*
> *For's Schulhaus an der Krick.*

But I must stop rambling around in this peculiar philology, and get on with my story. Some years later, when the first bloom of my interest in the Pennsylvania Germans had been rubbed off under pressure of more immediate concerns, I noticed that they were being visited with the curse of publicity. Fictioneers, mostly of the female persuasion, *Gott soll hüten*, were exploiting them in popular magazinedom. Reporters played them up by the side of their prowess in eating and their alleged prowess in witchcraft, the two accomplishments most likely to strike fire with the great American public. One or two cookbooks of dubious authenticity appeared. Then when lately the inhabitants of a certain district were had up in court for refusing to send their children to a State central school, I perceived that the Pennsylvania Germans were really in the news.

I did not read any of the fiction, nor did I care about the *Hexerei*, but the two items about food and schools attracted me. The mention of food set up a nagging persistent hankering for a certain native country-made product which I had sampled many years before. I am not naming it because it seems to be scarce as hens' teeth, and having at last found it I am happily on the inside track and propose to stay there; so any inquiry about it will merely waste postage.

Thus my interest in the Pennsylvania Germans livened up again. My hankering for the food-product would not subside, so I began to take measures. I wrote to the publisher of a book dealing largely with the region's cookery, asking him to sound out the young woman who wrote it; which he did, with no result. I wrote the chambers of commerce in the principal towns; the executive secretaries gave me names of some producers, to whom in turn I wrote without result. I then bethought me of my old friend Jeff Jones, who maintains a sales force in those parts; so I wrote him, suggesting that he turn his hellhounds loose to harry the whole countryside without respite, which I don't doubt he did, but they brought down no prey. At last I perceived that the matter required my personal attention. I determined to set forth in person and explore the counties of Lebanon and Lancaster with two objects in view. First, I would see what account of themselves the Pennsylvania Germans were actually giving. Second, I would find that food-product if it existed, whether in the heavens above those two counties, or on the earth beneath, or in the waters under the earth. The opportunity presenting itself, I went and was successful. I found the food-product, as I have already said, and bore it away in a burst of glory. I also found that the Pennsylvania Germans have a vast deal to say for themselves. One group especially excited my interest, and it is of them that I propose now to speak.

II

They are known as the Old Amish or House Amish. They are a split-off from the Mennonites, a religious body formed at Zurich early in the sixteenth century. In number, the Old Amish run to something between 8500 and 9000, and of these some 1500 are settled in the county of Lancaster, mostly on a stretch of rich farmland bordered by the Conestoga. They have been there since 1720, and their small rural communities grew up under odd names like Smoketown, Bird-in-hand, Blue Ball. I could get no reliable account of the origin of these names.

The Old Amish are reputed to be the best farmers in America, and a glance at their territory sets up a strong conviction that this is so. The Amishman is actually a farmer, not a manufacturer, like our large-scale single-crop producers. Nor is he a political farmer, of the kind whose perennial sorrows lie so close to the heart of Mr. Wallace. He cares nothing whatever for Mr. Wallace, and asks no political favors from anybody. His produce goes first to feed his family and his livestock. If any be left over, he takes it to the public markets at Lancaster; and by the way, if you want to see something which you could really call a public market, go to Lancaster. I never in my life saw so much superexcellent superelegant produce of all kinds clustered together as I saw there, and practically all of it was Amish produce. But speaking commercially, the Amishman's market trade is on the side; what he gets out of it is loose change—lagniappe. He is not a truck-gardener. After the needs of his family are provided for, after he has put down great store and abundance of beef products, pork products, dairy products, vegetable and cereal products, all of his own raising—then if he can pick up an odd dollar or two in the markets, well and good; but not before.

Judged by current standards, the Amishman has an unorthodox view of his mission in life. His one cash crop is tobacco. If he were a right-minded man, he would put down all the land he could get hold of in tobacco, and let his family eat out of tin cans. But in the first place, he does not want any more land than he and his family can work properly under their own steam. He is not keen on hired help, and sees nothing in sharecropping. Then further, he has only very vague and uncertain notions about tin cans; I suspect you might have to go quite a way to find a can-opener in an Amish household, or to find anybody who has ever seen one. For the Amishman, the idea of paying out good money for canned foodstuffs far inferior to what one can raise for oneself is one of those things that simply will not bear thinking about. Hence he limits his cash crop rigorously; it is strictly a side line, like his other market trade. It yields him plenty of money to go on with, for he needs hardly any, and he lets it go at that.

By sticking to this general policy for a couple of centuries, the Amish have worked themselves into an economic position that is pretty nearly impregnable. They have the real thing in "social security." Ten years ago, one of my town-dwelling friends wrote to a correspondent asking how Lancaster was doing under the depression. The correspondent telegraphed back, "What depression? There is no depression here." The Amish, putting it mildly, are exceeding well-to-do; or as the sinful would phrase it, they are rich as soap-grease. I have heard say that Lancaster County is the richest agricultural region in the world, and I believe it; richest, that is, in good hard available cash money that can be dug up on demand at any moment, out of the Amishman's pants pocket.

The Amish beat the New Deal's whole program of social security, hands down. They have the best form of old-age pension that can be devised; when you grow old you simply take things easy, and live *wie Gott in Frankreich* while your family carries on. No need for some officious nincompoop to come down from Washington and tell you how to do that. So also with "relief." No Amishman's name was ever yet on the relief roll of Lancaster County, and none ever will be. The Amishman does not waste a single bawbee on insurance, for he already has the best kind of insurance, on which he pays no premiums and his policy never expires. If lightning strikes his barn, his coreligionists in that district build him a new one; if he is ill, they help out with his work; if he dies untimely, they make arrangements to have things go on. No insurance company can compete with that.

He takes no oaths and signs no contracts or any form of written agreement, nor will he serve on juries or have anything to do with litigation; his religion forbids him all such. He lets his yea be yea and his nay nay, as the Bible commands, and he always keeps his given word. He is not a speculator or a borrower, and he does not hold public office. He is punctilious about taxes, paying the State's blackmail in full, and asking nothing in return but to be let alone—poor soul, as if that were not the very last thing the State would ever consent to do for anybody! The State lately foisted a grant of some $56,000 on the Old Amish for a PWA project in one of their townships, and they not only refused to accept it but appealed to the courts to have the noisome proposal nullified. It is no wonder that when this incredible miracle was reported at Washington the effect on the PWA personnel was devastating; fifteen fainted away, eleven went into convulsions, and three of them died. I have this on good authority.

III

The visitor does not have to look too closely to see what principle, what general theory of life, is at work here to bring this exemplary state of things about. It is religion. The Old Amish have the record of sticking longer and more faithfully to the original tenets, customs, and practices of their religion than any other Christian body in America; and it is this fidelity which has brought them where they are. This obviously says something for the Old Amish themselves, individually and collectively; but it also says something rather handsome for their religion. In the matter of getting results —and this is what all variants of religion presumably aim at —the Old Amish variant seems valid enough to stand up under the fire of criticism's most heftiest *Blitzkrieg*. Like the provisions of the Levitical law, its tenets, apparently arbitrary as many of them are, turn out to have a surprising deal of sound science and sound common sense behind them. In this they furnish material for advantageous comparison with the tenets and practices of other religious bodies. They will not, and should not, suggest to these bodies a wholesale taking over and substitution of Old Amish tenets and practices to displace their own. They do suggest, however, that if the other bodies want results comparable with those the Old Amish get under their conditions, they should make whatever modifications and displacements are appropriate to bringing them about under their own conditions.

The Old Amish believe that the agrarian life is the one most in accord with the Scriptures. This is their fundamental tenet; it merely puts a religious sanction on the agrarian doctrine held by Turgot, Benjamin Franklin, and above all by Mr. Jefferson. The Amishman's logic of it is that man is a land-animal; God made him so. He derives his sustenance wholly from the land, and every kind and form of wealth that exists or can exist is producible only by the application of labor and capital to land; God made this arrangement. Therefore the more direct the mode of this application, the better and simpler becomes the fulfillment of God's will.

Now, whatever one may think of the theological side of this reasoning, the economic side of it is sound to the core. It is the basic position of fundamental economics, and there is no sophistry by which one can squirm away from it. But for the Amish the theological side is also sound, and they are strong on it; it sums up pretty much all the dogmatic theology the Amish have. They are probably a little weak on economic theory, but they are strong on the theological rationale of their agrarianism. It is the controlling principle of their lives. The result is that under this control their practice of sound agrarian economics has made them a solvent, stable, self-respecting people, as prosperous as any in the land and certainly the most independent; and it has also confirmed in them the sterling character and sterling moral qualities to which I have alluded.

Perhaps—I put it tentatively—perhaps this is about all that should be expected from this combination of forces. It is a highly respectable showing, to say the very least of it. I am told there is complaint against organized Christianity as being "out of touch with practical life" and therefore so dissatisfying that the churches are losing ground—well, here is one variant of organized Christianity, at any rate, which surely does not come under that censure.

Artemus Ward said the trouble with Napoleon was that he tried to do too much, and did it. Something like this may be the trouble with organized Christianity at large. The expectations it puts upon human nature may be a little excessive. The ultimate secular aim it proposes for the individual may not be quite simple and definite enough, and its confessional constructions may involve more metaphysics than the average mind can comfortably take in. I feel free to suggest this because I myself am far too simple-minded to get the drift of such apologetic literature, even of the most modern type, as has come my way. When I ask myself just what it is driving at, and what it proposes for me to drive at, I am wholly at a loss for an answer.

In these respects the Old Amish variant is exceptional. On its confessional side it has next to nothing, no formal creed, no metaphysical formulas, no elaborate theology. On its secular side, its aim for the individual is simple, clear, and moderate. Its counsels and assistances are all directed towards the two-fold end of making him an upright man and a first-class farmer. Beyond this they seem not to go. Judging by results, one would think that the rest of organized Christianity might profit by analogous—not the same, or similar, but analogous —simplifications, both of confessional content and practical intention.

All the prescriptions, customs, and practices which the Old Amish variant enforces tend towards the same end, even those which, as I have said, seem petty and arbitrary. They have actually the character and sanction of religious ritual, and there is no trouble about understanding their full and exact import. With the best will in the world, one can hardly say so much for such other variants of organized Christianity as I am acquainted with. For instance, in the November *Atlantic* Dr. Bell cites "one of the world's most harassed statesmen" as saying, "I could not live, I think . . . if I could not go to Mass. I assist several times a week." This devotion is all very well and highly commendable, but when this harassed statesman goes on to account for his devotion to this ritual practice in terms of what accrues from it (*mea culpa*, maybe *maxima culpa; prava et turpissima culpa,* if you like— however, there it is) I don't understand one single word of what he is talking about.

On the other hand, I get the bearing of the Amishman's ritual prescriptions instantly and with no trouble at all. They all aim, as I have said, at making him an upright man and a good farmer; and anybody knows sufficiently well what a good farmer is and what an upright man is, and what qualities go into their making. Moreover, one can hardly fail to see that if conduct be three-fourths of life, and if religion be supposed to bear at all on conduct, the very simplicity, clearness, and directness of the Amishman's prescriptions, their strict avoidance of trying to do too much, are decidedly advantageous in respect of conduct, by comparison with the more indeterminate and apparently unrelated prescriptions laid down by other variants of organized Christianity. For instance, while Dr. Bell's harassed statesman may be an exception, I never knew or heard of a modern statesman, harassed or otherwise, who would boggle for an instant at lying like a hundred devils, if some political exigency required it of him; nor one who would not on like occasion break his word at a moment's notice, connive at any form of violence and crime, or act the part of an arrant swindler. The Amishman will do none of these things under any circumstances. Thus while religion's higher satisfactions such as the harassed statesman speaks of, whatever those are, may be inaccessible to the Amishman, he plods his way throughout the whole broad area of conduct with the firm step of a pretty tolerably well accredited citizen; and this, I repeat, no modern statesman that I know or ever heard of seems either able to do or even notably desirous of doing. The Amishman quite literally "lives by his religion," and his religion seems to be a workable one to live by. At any rate, he does not turn to it, or return to it, from motives of weakness, disillusionment, or fear. In this respect he appears to have a decided advantage over the reclaimed brethren Dr. Bell cites in his admirable article.

Coming now to less recondite matters, the Old Amish get

a little "edge" even on the Quakers, in not having any churches. They meet for worship in their houses, taking them in turn throughout the district. They have no stated ministry. Each district chooses its minister by lot from among its own number, to serve for a year. He has no special training; every Amishman is presumed to be qualified for a job of such simplicity, and no doubt is. He is not paid one single picayune. These economical arrangements keep down the overhead, thereby wholly doing away with the need for ministerial salesmanship, advertising, canvassing for new members, and all other money-raising devices—a need which appears most seriously, often exclusively, to preoccupy other Christian communities.

There is a sound idea here. If you want to "purify politics," whether Church politics or secular politics, begin by taking the money out of it. You won't have to do much else; human nature will do the rest. It is exactly Lincoln Steffens's idea of fixing the responsibility for the Fall of Man. Some blame Adam, while others put the blame on Eve; Steffens put it on the apple. If the apple had not been there everything would have gone smoothly. Obviously, then, the thing to do in like circumstances is to take away the apple. If you do this you can't have any trouble, and this is what the Old Amish have done, thereby giving evidence of a great brain and a level head.

By this device they have closed up every loophole against professionalism. Rapid rotation in unpaid office, combined with absence of all special training, is death on the development of a priestly class. Sacerdotalism does not stand a dog's chance with the Old Amish; and the elaborate metaphysical *Aberglaube* of its associated sacramentalism stands no better chance. All this seems to suggest an opportunity for further simplification on the part of other Christian bodies. It is surely a fair question whether a competent practice of religion calls for quite as much apparatus, metaphysical and physical, as the main body of organized Christianity has constructed and is trying, none too successfully, to keep in running order. There need be, and should be, no thought of taking over the Old Amish pattern as it stands; yet no well-ordered mind should be above looking it over, on the chance of finding food for profitable thought.

Like orthodox Jews and Roman Catholics, the Old Amish send their children to schools of their own, to avoid contaminating contacts. They do not educate their children beyond the eighth grade, in the belief that this comprises all the book learning that a good farmer needs. There is much to be said for this view, and everything to be said for Mr. Jefferson's further view that this is as much as any but the very rarely exceptional child can use to any good purpose. America is now paying enormous amounts of margin on its cat-and-dog investments in a type of citizen "whose education is far too much for his abilities," as the Duke of Wellington said. Amish children may not enter the professions or the white-collar vocations, and this without prejudice to either; if, for instance, the Amishman has occasion to employ a physician, he gets the best one he can find and ungrudgingly pays him top prices. The only point is that in pursuance of the will of God those children are to stay on the land, and should be learning how to work the paternal acreage with love and reverence as well as skill. An Amish boy who wants to go to college and then take up a profession may of course do so, but not by easy gravitation. He must break with his religion, tradition, and family; and if his call is loud enough, and if he has grit enough to scrabble over this three-barred obstruction, the chances are that he is the sort to succeed. One cannot be sure but that this is as it should be, for we are discovering that the way to a desirable thing can be made altogether too easy. I am told, however, that the Amish children very seldom break over the traces, and one can easily see good reason why this should be so. They are already booked at birth for inheritance in about the soundest going concern in the United States, so why leave a bone for a shadow? They will always eat, and eat mighty well, always be well-clad, well-housed. They will never lose their jobs, never worry about their wives and children wanting bread, never punch a clock, truckle to a gang-boss, or scuffle for a living against cut-throat competition. They will always be able to look the world in the face and think and say exactly what they dam' well please about anything and anybody. Isn't that pretty much the old-time American ideal?

The Old Amish house themselves well, and keep their houses with the most painstaking neatness, but they have no central heating, their furniture is sparse and simple, and they have no ornaments. They use no electricity, thus escaping the distractions of the telephone, radio, telegraph, and motion picture. They do not use automobiles, but are finished experts with the horse and buggy; many, probably most of them, have never been farther away from home than the county town. They wear always the same cut of clothes, as distinctive as a uniform, with no adornment of any kind, not even buttons; their coats are fastened with hooks and eyes. If someone appears in their midst wearing buttoned garments, he is known at once as a "stylisher," and is given more or less of a wide berth. All these are religious observances. As can be easily seen, their aim is to encourage thrift and a wholesome simplicity of living, to promote domestic and communal solidarity, and to hit the golden mean between too much ease and comfort and too little. However rigorous and niggling such regulations may appear to us, it is a mistake to regard them as bearing heavily on their votaries, or to regard the Amish as a "stubborn, fierce and isolated people," as Matthew Arnold describes the Jews of early days. On the contrary, they have excellent humor, are fond of fun, and are extremely sociable and jolly among themselves; not, however, with strangers. They amuse themselves, as they do all things, simply and heartily; the lighter side of their life seems to be about what it was with their progenitors living in the Pfalz; or indeed, pretty much what it was with our own progenitors living in America not so many years ago.

IV

In studying any order of fauna one gets some impressions less agreeable than others. I got a few from the Amish that I thought were hardly worth carrying away with me, so I was glad to forget them. What did me a great and lasting good was to see what I had come to think existed nowhere in America, a people with a clear strong sense of the *ne quid nimis*, and a resolute determination to live by that sense. I was among them for only a short time, and saw their life only from outside; they are not partial to strangers. But even so, it was a cheering and hope-inspiring experience to touch the fringes of a well-to-do, prosperous, hard-working society which does not believe in too much money, too much land, too much impedimenta, too much ease, comfort, schooling, mechanization, aimless movement, idle curiosity; which does not believe in too many labor-saving devices, gadgets, gimcracks; and which has the force of character— fed and sustained by a type of religion which seems really designed to get results—the force of sterling character, I say, to keep itself well on the safe lee side of all such excesses.

ADVERTISING AND
LIBERAL LITERATURE

No doubt the advertising policies of periodicals have sins of their own to answer for, for the power of the advertiser is the power of patronage and can be easily abused. But those who complain of the bad reaction of advertising upon writers, especially upon radical writers, may get a certain consolation, whatever it amounts to, from remembering that advertising originally liberated the profession of writing and made it respectable and attractive. It took the writer off his patron's staircase and invested him with a larger independence and self-respect, insured his maintenance and got him better wages for his work. It was the radical writer, too, who reaped the largest advantage; in fact, one might fairly say that advertising has been the most important single factor in the promotion of liberal literature.

The pursuit of this clew is interesting. As far as I know, the first advertisement ever printed was a book-ad that appeared in 1647. But the real history of advertising begins for our purposes eighteen years later with the establishment of the *Oxford Gazette* on November 7, 1665.

This was an official paper, the mouthpiece of the court of King Charles II. It was published twice a week on a single sheet about seven inches by ten, or approximately the size of a standard magazine page; printed on both sides in two columns, carrying about five hundred words to the column or two thousand words to the issue. Being published under royal auspices, it had, of course, the most pronounced editorial "slant" on all the news of those parlous times. It is doubtful whether anything in our day can match the industrious twisting and garbling and straightaway lying by which this newspaper bolstered the royalist cause.

Fox Bourne says that this was "almost the only newspaper allowed to King Charles's subjects till near the end of his reign." Hence, obviously, the publisher did not need to worry about circulation. He had all there was. Between the Licensing Act and the censorship, he had easy going. Furthermore, as he operated under patronage, he was independent of advertising; and, in fact, as long as he had the field to himself, he carried practically no advertising except court-notices. In early issues I saw only a few book-ads, some advertisements of runaway apprentices and one for a lost dog. When the court moved from Oxford to London, the paper took the name of the *London Gazette* with the issue of Feb. 4, 1669. A couple of years later a few more miscellaneous ads appear, and by 1680 they occasionally amount to as much as a column; but one may fairly say that this paper ran a dozen years without any general advertising business worth mentioning.

At this time the people of England were getting more or less uncertain and captious about the Stuart regime, and by 1682 some publisher seems to have thought that the insurgent spirit was strong enough to support a newspaper; so in that year, after the *Gazette* had enjoyed a clear field for seventeen years, a privately owned competitor called the *Mercury* appeared. Its policy was radical and progressive; its method a fine monochrome study in pure yellow. The editor —some earlier and nameless Hearst—did his work in a style that must remain the delight and the despair of imitators. In his earlier issues he set forth a declaration asserting his independence of court politics and influential persons. He laid down this challenge in the language of eighteen-carat insurgency, and seasoned it with urbane and salty innuendoes against the policy of the court paper. He closed his prospectus with the promise to stick by his insurgent programme and get out his paper as long as his undertaking was supported or "until stopt by Authority."

Now what enabled him to do this? Advertising. There is no doubt of it, the analysis of his columns shows it. He ran more advertising in his first month than his subsidized contemporary ran in three years. His first issue carried long advertisements of two books that were a direct appeal to the insurgent spirit. One of these books was a work on religious philosophy, espousing the Puritan or Presbyterian doctrine and antagonizing the political alliance of church and State which was fostered by the Stuarts and Archbishop Laud. It does not seem any great piece of radicalism in these days, but it was tremendous for its time. The other book was a history of "the Adventures and Discoveries of several famous Men" (among others, Sir Walter Raleigh), chronicling and commending the achievements of independent adventure and the come-outer spirit. Several real-estate advertisements appear in the same issue, and one of James Maddox, or Madox, the name being spelled both ways, an undertaker who seems to have worked out a new embalming process. Maddox's advertisements ran consistently through the whole life of the *Mercury* and he used large space; so the process doubtless gave satisfaction.

The second issue of the *Mercury* contained a whole column of advertising, as much as any single issue of the *Gazette* came to in twelve years, and it presents the first specimen, as far as I know, of classified ads. The real-estate ads increase in number; and in the third issue some enterprising broker is quick to take a preferred position immediately under the real-estate classification, informing people in so many words that if they have any real-estate to dispose of they might better let him attend to it personally than trust to hit-or-miss advertising in a newspaper. There is a certain irony about this. He promises privacy, uses a three-star run-around to attract attention, and altogether makes the impression of a good, lively business-getter.

There are some peculiar features to these real-estate ads. First, it is rather remarkable that there are so many of them and that the terms so often indicate a great sacrifice. One place, for instance, costing £10,000 to build the house alone, will be let go in a lump for £4,000. Rentals are relatively as low as sales prices. It would seem that the troubled state of politics was suggesting to people of quality that they should pull out of their real-estate holdings and get ready to jump. This view is somewhat supported by the fact that these ads are nearly always rather more than anonymous; that is, the advertiser not only suppresses his name, but usually he does not even disclose the location of his property. One is struck, too, by the very modern way these ads have of talking about the climate. One after another keeps saying, "as good air as will be found anywhere within five miles of London," etc. Now as far as natural climate goes, there could be little choice in air at any place within five miles of the London of that day—or of this, for that matter. Hence it would seem that although the factory system did not come in until nearly one hundred years after, there might have been something of a smoke problem even then.

The *Mercury's* advertising rate is not known; but from calculations based on a financial statement of the *Spectator* about 1712, at the time the newspapers were all taxed out of existence by the monstrous and crushing levy of 1s per ad of any length, it seems reasonable to believe that the advertisements in the second issue of the *Mercury* paid for its paper, printing, and distribution. If so, the twelfth issue, carrying one and an eighth columns, and the seventeenth, carrying one and a half, represent considerable "velvet."

The truly miscellaneous character of the *Mercury's* advertising, as compared with that of its subsidized competitor, may be inferred from a single specimen. On September 8, 1682, a barber named Robert Whiting offers for sale—

Many hundreds of Natural Rarities, as Alegators, Crocadiles, Goanes, Armadels, Dolphins, King-Crabs, Snakes, Pellecans, Bugalogs, and all manner of Shells, Fish and Sea-Eggs.

In the eighteenth issue appears our true friend, our faithful stand-by, the sheet-anchor of newspaper advertising—the patent-medicine man. He makes his initial bow modestly, with a gentle panegyric on the virtues of Spruce Beer, a medicinal drink. A few issues later, however, namely, on September 19, 1682, he comes forth in all his war-paint and feathers in praise of the True Spirit of Scurvygrass.

Many imagine that the psychology of advertising is a modern discovery and that all the tricks of the trade have been worked out of whole cloth in the last quarter of a century or some such matter. To such I earnestly recommend a careful analysis of the *Mercury's* advertisement of the True Spirit of Scurvygrass. It will encourage them by showing that even if we are now no better than we ought to be, we are at all events no worse than them of old time.

First, the True Spirit of the Scurvygrass is offered to a suffering public because "all are troubled with the Scurvy more or less." This is an interesting statement, and calculated to start the guileless prowling for symptoms. It has a good force of suggestion; we have all perused more modern advertisements similarly equipped—yea, and in our own flesh have felt each horrid exponent and token rise responsive to the roll-call! Next follows a trade-mark warning, and a plain hint of the prevalence of rebating, or giving dealers a rake-off for pushing one's goods:

Many for Lucre's sake make something which they call Spirit of Scurvygrass, etc., and to promote it both in Town and Country give threepence or a Groat in a Glass to such as will boast and cry it up and dispraise far better than what they sell.

Beware of imitations! Refuse substitutes! None other is genuine! There is nothing particularly new about this, either; we have heard of it before, even to the rebating.

Then follows a courteous and ingenious effort to break the news gently, for which everyone is properly grateful, of course, but yet in spite of it—in spite of the tender solicitude for the Meaner sort, in spite of the transparent purity of the designs upon the Rich in behalf of their Poor Neighbours— one can not help noticing that this remedy was sold at what appears, for those days, a rousing price:

In order that the Meaner sort may easily reach it and the Rich be induced to help their Poor Neighbours, it is or- dered to be sold for Sixpence a Glass.

About 1706 the patent-medicine ads begin to crowd all others out of the newspapers—a sure indication that they could and did pay a higher rate. No wonder! No wonder, either, that they were the only ads to survive the imposition of the devastating tax on advertisements some six years later. The True Spirit of Scurvygrass at sixpence a throw in a coun- try where all are troubled with the Scurvy more or less, must have been a moneymaker. Its extremely wide range of thera- peutic virtue also no doubt helped its sale. It would cure anything—anything. When the advertiser gets really warmed up to his work he rises to the strain of Dr. Dulcamara in the *Elisir d'Amore:*

Upon trial you will perceive this Spirit to root out the Scurvy and all its Dependents; as also to help Pains in the Head, Stomach, Shortness of Breath, Dropsies, lost Appetite, Faintness, Vapours, Wind in any Part, Worms, Itching, Yellowness, Spots, etc. Loose Teeth and Decayed Gums are helped by rubbing them with a few drops, as also any Pain in the Limbs. . . .

And so forth and so on. A dose of the True Spirit was a potshot at the whole category of ills that flesh is heir to. If it didn't get what it went after, it would bag something else. It never fired any blank cartridges.

The True Spirit of Scurvygrass was first advertised in the *Mercury* on September 19, 1682. In the next issue, September 22, under an ad for a lost gold watch, appears an ad of imposing length—a whole half column of it—proclaiming—

the Old and True Way of Practicing Physick, revived by Dr. Tho. Kirleus, His Majesty's Sworn Physician in Ordinary, presented by the Rt. Hon., the Earl of Shaftesbury, and approved by the most competent judges of the Art, the College of Physicians, under their Hands and Seal.

Thus it appears that, like his latter-day brethren who advertise, Dr. Tho. Kirleus was "a graduate physician in regular standing." But whatever his professional status may have been, Dr. Tho. was a master of the art of advertising. Within the space of forty-two words—only forty-two words—this remarkable man manages to crowd nearly every trick of the modern medicine-monger:

he gives his Opinion for nothing to any that writes or comes to him, and safe Medicines for little, but to the Poor for Thanks; and in all Diseases where the Cure may be discerned, he expects nothing until it be cured.

Analyze this prospectus. Consultation gratis; consultation by mail; "harmless vegetable remedy"; free treatment for those unable to pay; no cure, no pay. Only one thing is missing; and it is supplied in the very next sentence by the swift and masterly hand of Dr. Tho.:

Of the Gout he cured himself ten years since, when crippled with Knots in his Hands and Feet, but now able to go with any Man of his age ten or twenty Miles.

There we have it! That last touch rounds out the advertisement, makes it perfect, and establishes an open channel and communication with the enterprise of our modern age! "One who has suffered from rheumatism for seventeen years, etc., etc., will send by mail, etc., etc." How pleasant and restful and thoroughly at home it makes one feel to be rewarded with finds like this among the dust and ashes of the lamented past, before the era of commercialism had set in!

Dr. Tho. Kirleus was a persistent and consistent advertiser, but subsequent indications show that while he became prosperous, he did not live long to enjoy his triumphs. His affairs went on, however, managed by competent hands and directed by heads that had thoroughly learned the value of advertising, as we shall shortly see.

The *Mercury* passed out of existence in 1686, whether from natural causes or "stopt by Authority" I do not know. The next insurgent paper that I examined for advertising was the *Review*, established by Daniel Defoe in 1700, fourteen years after the end of the *Mercury*. As a muckraker, the author of *Robinson Crusoe* was entitled to the red ribbon. He knew every political and social situation in England; he knew the strength and weakness of every element in its civilization;

he had an unfailing instinct for the psychological moment in journalism; he knew just what to write about and when to play it up, and how to use the right word in the right place with a calm and deadly accuracy that never failed. Although the actors in those scenes have long since passed into infamous oblivion, it is yet a perennial pleasure to turn to Daniel's pages and watch him kerosene some mongrel politician's coat-tails and apply the match.

Naturally, these activities attracted unfavorable attention, so that Defoe seems occasionally to have stood from under. He speaks in one place of editing his paper sometimes at a distance of 400 miles from London. He had trouble also with the news companies; the "Hawkers or Shops," he says, would not handle his goods—too much sedition in them, likely. He had, however, a London agent named Mathews who seems to have been a hustler, so between them they were able to get the paper pretty well distributed in spite of official opposition and the timidity of newsdealers. The people stood by Defoe, and in four years' time he was able to get out a twenty-eight page monthly supplement, a real magazine, the precursor of our present monthly periodicals. This contained many modern magazine features; one of which, however— the write-up of some current event in excellent Latin verse —would probably not get very far in these times.

All this, again, was kept up by advertising. In 1710 Defoe speaks of financing a new project by subscription "until it shall be able to support itself," but the estimated cost of paper and presswork leaves little doubt that at the outset it was rather more than covered by advertising. There is some reason for believing that the advertising rate was based upon circulation, for there is record of one paper published about this time that gave away a thousand copies of one issue as "padding." This, however, is only conjecture. Either Defoe himself or his agent Mathews was what we should now call a crackerjack solicitor, for it is in Defoe's paper that we particularly notice the tendency to crowd out the low-priced ads in favor of those that could and would bring up the rate, such as cosmetics patent medicines, trusses, and goods in the luxury class, in which there was presumably a very large margin of profit. It appears from Defoe's ads that many of these goods, especially patent medicines, were handled by booksellers.

The first illustrated ad appears in 1706—a rude wood cut of some trusses that a manufacturer was putting on the market. Defoe himself had little use for drugs or doctors; in one place he says editorially that "what the ancients fabulously reported of Pandora's box is strictly true of the doctor's packet; and that it contains in it the seeds and principles of all diseases." Defoe evidently had no qualms about offending his best advertisers. Nor yet had Steele. Steele, in the *Spectator*, curses quacks as impostors and murderers, while tranquilly advertising probably the very worst of them; and from 1708 on Defoe's paper carried hardly anything but a line of patent-medicine advertising like this:

All Melancholy and Hypochondriacal Distempers of Mind with strange Fears, Dismal Apprehensions, great Oppression and Sinking of Spirit (little understood and seldom Cured by any common Means). Also Sick-Fits, Faintings, Tremblings and other Disorders arising from Vapours, etc., are successfully Cured (with God's blessing) by a Physician well experienced and of more than 20 Years' Practice in these deplorable Cases.

"With God's blessing" is certainly a very handsome proviso, and does the writer credit. A similar pious concession appears in another advertisement of the same issue, which I quote for the sake of another familiar trick of the trade, namely, the "sealed package," which I believe makes its first appearance here:

Most excellent strengthening Pills, which give certain Help in all Pains or Weakness of the Back (either in Man or Woman) occasioned by a Strain or Wrench or any other cause; being a sure Remedy (under God) in such cases for Cure. At 3s a Box containing 8 Doses (sealed up) with printed Directions.

We see also from Defoe's paper that by 1707 a good deal of the charitable bread cast on the waters by our fine old friend Dr. Tho. Kirleus had begun to float back. Dr. Tho. had meanwhile been gathered to his fathers, but the business was carried on by his son's widow, who, for consistency and explicitness of advertising, might be regarded as the Lydia E. Pinkham of that bygone day. She recommends his medicines for a variety of disorders not contemplated by the good old man's original advertisement which we found running in the *Mercury*, and she specifies some of them with a Hogarthian directness which we must not quote. We find that—

Mary Kirleus, the Widow of John Kirleus, son of Dr. Tho. Kirleus, a sworn Physician in Ordinary to King Charles II., sells (rightly prepared) his famous Drink and Pills; experienced above 50 years to cure all Ulcers, Sores, Scabs, Itch, Scurf, Scurvies, Leprosies . . . These incomparable Medicines need no Words to express their Virtues . . . In Compassion to the distressed, she will deal according to the Patient's Ability. The Drink is 3s the Quart, the Pill 1s the Box with Directions and Advice Gratis.

"Above 50 years"—truly a long time in the little life of men! John, too, we perceive, has gone—gone to rejoin Dr. Tho. But Mary is still with us, very much alive and on the job!

Yes, whatever our impatience with the control of periodicals by force of advertising patronage, it is well to remember the immense emancipating power exercised upon writers of the past by this same force. Advertising enabled the London *Mercury* to come out as a red-hot insurgent paper and do an enormous service to liberal thought, when nothing else in the world could have held it up over one issue. It emancipated writers from the more personal and irresponsible sort of patronage that controlled the *Gazette,* for instance. It encouraged them to say what they pleased, even to the extent of abusing their best advertisers, as Steele did, and Defoe. It was advertising that unchained Defoe and galvanized his elbow and pointed his quill, and enabled him to do tremendous service to the cause of liberalism at a time when it most needed service.

And even to-day perhaps things are not as bad as they might be. I am not able to discuss the plight of the professional writer or the propagandist, but there is another class of writers who seem to me still under a very considerable obligation to advertising. I refer to the large number of what one might call marginal minds, who have no idea of writing for a living, but who write a good deal, merely to express themselves, merely to say what they think, while getting their living some other way. Advertising, by maintaining a great body of periodical literature, furnishes these the opportunity to get into print; and thus, out of this mass of more or less mediocre and unprofessional self-expression there occasionally emerges one who finds he has a gift for it. Then, as advertising has enabled him to discover himself, so it is advertising that enables him to develop himself, that gives him the encouraging and almost necessary practice in seeing himself in print. So while its bearing may have changed somewhat, one may still say that advertising is performing its historic public service in liberating and stimulating the potential writer.

HENRY GEORGE:
UNORTHODOX AMERICAN

A DEPRESSION was on in the year 1864. In those days depressions did not go by their Latin name as a rule, except when people wanted to put on airs about them, but were called by the simple English name of hard times. This streak of hard times lay very heavily on the Pacific Coast. It was aggravated by a great drouth that burned up the grain crop and pasturage, and killed most of the cattle on the ranches. There was no business in farming or ranching, industries were closed down, and commerce was at a dead halt.

At this time Henry George was twenty-five years old, living miserably in San Francisco, where, after a long struggle with misfortune, he had set up in a small way as a job printer. He had a wife and child, and his wife was shortly to give birth again. He could get no work, whether at printing or anything else, nor could he ask help from any one, for all the people he knew were wretchedly poor. Long afterward, speaking of this period, he said that as things went from bad to worse—

> I came near starving to death, and at one time I was so close to it that I think I should have done so but for the job of printing a few cards which enabled us to buy a little corn meal. In this darkest time in my life my second child was born.

When this event happened he had no money, no food, no way to provide his wife with any care; he was alone in a bare lodging with a helpless suffering woman and a new-born baby. In a desperate state of mind he left the house and took to the last resort of the destitute.

I walked along the street and made up my mind to get money from the first man whose appearance might indicate that he had it to give. I stopped a man, a stranger, and told him I wanted five dollars. He asked what I wanted it for. I told him that my wife was confined and that I had nothing to give her to eat. He gave me the money. If he had not, I think I was desperate enough to have killed him.

Henry George had seen depressions before. When he was sixteen years old he saw one in Australia, where he lay in port for a month as foremast-boy on an old East Indiaman sailing out of New York for Melbourne and Calcutta. There he found times "very hard ashore, thousands with nothing to do and nothing to eat." Two years later, in 1857, another depression threw him out of work in Philadelphia and sent him wandering to the Pacific Coast. After 1864, too, he was to be wrecked by still another depression, when the appalling hard times which followed the panic of 1873 broke up in succession two newspaper enterprises which had employed him, and he was once more set adrift and penniless.

Thus it was that the question occurred to him, why do these depressions happen? Why should there be any hard times? Nobody seemed to know. People took depressions as they took tuberculosis or typhoid, or as people in the Middle Ages took the bubonic plague, as something bound to happen, something that had to be put up with. They had always happened about once every so often, undoubtedly would always go on happening, and that was that. Yet in the nature of things there seemed no reason why they should happen. There was plenty of natural opportunity for everybody, plenty of everything that anybody could possibly need. The country was not poor and overpopulated—far from it. On the contrary, it was fabulously rich and had only a thin and straggling population. Nevertheless, every so often, with a strange regularity, hard times came around and vast masses of the people were left without work and without bread.

There must be some reason for this which no one had as yet discovered, and Henry George made up his mind that if he lived he would find out what it was.

Somehow he did manage to live. By one means or another he got over the peak of his greatest distress, and four years later, in the winter of 1868, he came from California to New York on an errand for a newspaper. He was then not quite thirty years old, and did not even yet have a dollar in his pocket that he could call his own. New York showed him something brand-new in his experience. Up to this time he had not been in a position to see any great show of inequality in the distribution of wealth. Life was simple in the Philadelphia of his boyhood days, and in the rough and new California of his youth one person lived much like another. But now, in the New York of 1868, he saw our western Palmyra in all the shoddy glory of its post-war period, and by all accounts it must have been a most dreadful sight, as repulsive as the pens of Dickens and George William Curtis pictured it. Shoddy riches, shoddy show, shoddy ideals and taste, shoddy people—and on the other hand, whole populations of troglodyte slum-dwellers living at an almost inconceivable depth of wretchedness and degradation.

Years afterward George said that here "I saw and recognized for the first time the shocking contrast between monstrous wealth and debasing want." What was the cause of it? Again, nobody seemed to know. Like depressions and plagues, it was taken as part of the regular order of nature. It had always existed in large commercial and industrial centers, apparently it was bound always to exist, and it seemed to be just another one of the things that had to be put up

with. There was no cure for it, so far as anybody knew. All
that could be done was to take some of the curse off it by
charity of one sort or another, and this was being done; in
fact, it was beginning to be organized on a large scale, more
lavishly perhaps than in any other country.

Nevertheless, George reasoned with himself, the thing had
to have a cause, for nothing in nature ever happens without
a cause. If that cause could be found, a cure might be found;
but trying to deal with an effect without knowing anything
about its cause would be mere fumbling in the dark. Here,
then, was a second question, to which George pledged his
lifetime for an answer. The first question was, what is the
cause—not any superficial and apparent cause, but the true
fundamental cause—of recurrent industrial depressions? The
second question was, what is the true fundamental cause of
the enormous inequality in the distribution of wealth?

George succeeded in answering these two questions to his
own satisfaction while he was still a comparatively young
man. This was the only success he ever had in his life; whatever else he touched failed. His one success, however, such
as it was, led him through one of the strangest and most remarkable careers ever achieved in America, or for that matter, in the world.

II

In principle, as the politicians say, Henry George's boyhood followed the course laid out by the story-books that
used to be written around the romance of American life. He
did not exactly run away from school or run away to sea,
but he did what came to the same thing. He served notice on
his parents so firmly that they decided to let him have his own
way. In the matter of schooling they perhaps thought it was
just as well, for he seems to have been an all-round failure at
any kind of book-learning. Between the ages of six and four-

teen he tried his luck at four different schools, three of them private schools, and all of them first-rate as schools went in those days—and probably they went about as well then as they do now—but he was not worth his salt at any of them. He worried through the grammar grades, entered the high school, stuck at it almost half a year, and then struck his colors for good and all; he never had another day's schooling.

He said afterward, rather austerely, that in his half year at the high school he "was idle, and wasted time." He may have done so, but if he did it was exceptional, for as boy or man he was never shiftless or dissipated, but always a hard worker, with an uncommon amount of intellectual curiosity and scientific imagination. The worst of him was that he was hasty and impatient, and of a roaming, restless disposition which probably made his parents think that his best hope of getting any kind of discipline lay in the forecastle, and that since he wanted most of all to go to sea, it might be the best thing for him if they should let him go.

One matter connected with this period in his life is worth notice. When he was forty years old, he suddenly appeared before the world as the master of a superb English prose style, a style that very few writers have equalled. Everybody of any literary experience at once began to wonder where in the world he could have got it, and how, and when. His record was open. With virtually no schooling, he had been a sailor, a typesetter, a tramp, a peddler, printer, shopclerk, newspaperman, weigher in a rice-mill, ship's steward, inspector of gas meters, gold-seeker, farm laborer. There was clearly nothing in any of these pursuits, or in all of them put together, to raise a man's prose style to that high level. How did he come by it?

It is usually said that he learned to write by hard practice, mainly between 1865 and 1870, and it is true that his actual career as a writer began in that period. But he did not get his style then, for he always had it. Scraps of a diary that he kept on shipboard show that he wrote the same clear, precise, and beautiful English at seventeen that he did at forty. For example:

> Wed. 11. I was roused out of a sound sleep at twelve o'clock to come on deck and keep my watch. On turning out I found a great change in the weather. The wind had shifted to N.W., and come out cold and fierce. The ship was running dead before it in a S.E. direction, making about eight or nine knots an hour. After keeping a cold and dreary watch until four A.M., we were relieved. . . . In the afternoon all hands were engaged in getting the anchors on the forecastle and securing them for a long voyage. The colour of the sea is green on sounding, the shade varying according to the depth of water, and a beautiful blue outside; and so very clear that objects can be seen at a great depth.

Or this, which any critic would pass unquestioned as having been written by R. H. Dana:

> The wind, which had been strong from aft the day before, during the middle watch died away and was succeeded by a calm until eight A.M., when a stiff breeze from the south sprang up, accompanied by shadows of rain. At twelve M. all hands were called to reef. While reefing the fore-topsail, the parrel of the yard gave way, causing a great deal of trouble and keeping all hands from dinner. It was two-thirty P.M. before our watch got below to their plum-duff, which had been allowed in honour of the day. The rest of the day was rainy, with wind constantly varying, keeping us hauling on the braces. Thus closed the most miserable Fourth of July that I have ever yet spent.

When a boy of seventeen turns off such English as that, day after day, for his own eye only, no one should be surprised at what he does for the public eye at forty. It is not easy to hit just that blend of precision, clearness, simplicity and grace—let the reader try it. George never wrote a sentence that needed a second reading to tell not only what it meant, but the only thing it could possibly mean, or be made to mean. In this respect he stands with the most formidable champion of the established order that he ever had to face— Professor Huxley—and with all its force of clearness and precision, his style has also a grace of warmth and color which Huxley's has not.

But as George himself would have said, a man's style must come from somewhere, it must have a cause. A person is not simply born knowing how to do that sort of thing. More probably he got it from the kind of English that he was brought up to hear and speak at home, and from his familiarity with the English of the Bible and the Book of Common Prayer. Such of the family's letters as exist are extremely well written, and his schoolmates and cronies—Bishop Henry C. Potter and his brother, Bishop Horstmann, James Morgan Hart, Doctor R. Heber Newton and his brother—were certainly bred to have a decent respect for their native tongue, so in all probability George heard excellent English from his infancy. His father was a vestryman of old St. Paul's, who brought up his children in the strict ways of old-style Evangelical Protestantism, with the result that Henry seems to have known the King James Version practically by heart, so that his own English may have been modelled, more or less consciously, on its narrative style.

He went to sea in April, 1855, and his voyage on the *Hindoo* lasted a year and two months. She was an old wooden affair of 600 tons, in none too good shape, bought second-hand for a kind of tramp service after twenty-five years of hard wear and tear as an East Indiaman. She went out of New

York in lumber for Melbourne. The record is that she carried half a million feet, which seems close to an overload for a ship of her tonnage—an awkward cargo, at any rate. She took a deal of tinkering, as the passage just quoted from George's journal shows. Before she was a week out her tiller broke in half, rotted at the core, but fortunately the sea was calm enough to let the crew fix tackles on the rudder to steer by, while the carpenter rigged a new gear. Except for incidents like this, and a few days' stretch of heavy weather in the Indian Ocean, the voyage was uneventful, enabling George to learn the sailor's trade in as easy circumstances, probably, as he could have had. His captain seems to have been a very good sort, who saw to it that the crew got as decent treatment as the state of the ship allowed.

George did not go ashore much, though the *Hindoo* lay off Melbourne nearly a month. He looked the town over once, and did not care for it. This was three years after the gold rush of 1852, and a "readjustment" had set in—in plain language, hard times—which made everything look down at the heel. All the people he saw were poor, idle, and dejected. Calcutta also disappointed him. He did his duty by the scenery up the river, finding it very fine, and he took in the features of native life that seemed quaint to an American eye, the bamboo huts, home-made earthenware, the strange shape of the river-boats, some of which, he wrote, "had sails to help them along, in which there were more holes than threads." He noticed the handsome country residences of the rich English living on both sides of the river, and also, by way of contrast, the number of corpses floating downstream in all stages of decomposition, covered with obscene black birds picking them to pieces. "The first one I saw filled me with horror and disgust," he wrote, "but like the natives, you soon cease to pay any attention to them."

Altogether it was not quite the India that a boy dreams of at a distance. He found it, as he afterwards said, "a land where the very carrion birds are more sacred than human life." A brief look at things ashore was enough for him, and when the *Hindoo* had got her thousand tons of rice aboard, he was glad to leave the land and go back on the open sea. He had sailor's blood in his veins, by his father's side of the family, two generations back, which may have given him something of the true sailor's virtuoso spirit. At the end of a year's voyage, although looking forward eagerly to seeing his family and friends in Philadelphia, he wrote in his journal, "Oh, that I had it to go over again."

The sea was not through with him, however. After the reunion with his people was over, the next thing was to cast about for something to do. His father got him a place with a printing firm to learn typesetting, where he stayed nine months, long enough to become a good journeyman compositor, and then quit in consequence of a row with his foreman. He had an offer from another firm, but the pay was nothing worth thinking of, and he did not take it. The depression of 1857 was coming on, and the few employers who had a place open were offering sweatshop terms. Finding that there was simply nothing doing in Philadelphia, he went to Boston, working his way on a topmast schooner that carried coal. There was nothing doing there either; so, on his return, attracted by reports of the fortunes being made on the Pacific Coast, he shipped on the lighthouse-tender *Shubrick*, which was going on the long voyage around the foot of South America, for service out of San Francisco.

While learning his new trade of typesetting in Philadelphia, he took lessons at night in penmanship and bookkeeping, with useful results. When his handwriting was fully formed, it was small and highly characteristic, but very clear and neat. Part of his father's idea in having him learn to set type was to improve his spelling. Like some other great writers, notably Count Tolstoy, he could not spell. This branch of the mechanics of writing seems to call for some obscure kind of natural gift or aptitude, which George never had. He thought typesetting helped him a little, but it could not have helped him much, for he misspelled even the commonest words all his life.

While he was working at the case, too, there happened one of those trivial incidents that turn out to be important in setting the course of one's life. He heard an old printer say that in a new country wages are always high, while in an old country they are always low. George was struck by this remark and on thinking it over, he saw that it was true. Wages were certainly higher in the United States than in Europe, and he remembered that they were higher in Australia than in England. More than this, they were higher in the newer parts than in the older parts of the same country—higher in Oregon and California, for instance, than in New York and Pennsylvania.

George used to say that this was the first little puzzle in political economy that ever came his way. He did not give it any thought until long after; in fact, he says he did not begin to think intently on any economic subject until conditions in California turned his mind that way. When finally he did so, however, the old printer's words came back to him as a roadmark in his search for the cause of industrial depressions, and the cause of inequality in the distribution of wealth.

III

Like all those who anticipated Horace Greeley's classic advice to young men, Henry George went west for quick money and plenty of it. He had no notion of mining, but of prospecting; that is to say, his idea was not to work a mine, but to pick up mineral land, and then either sell it or have it worked on shares with somebody who would do the actual mining. In short, as he would have phrased it in later years, his idea was to make his fortune by appropriating the economic rent of natural resources, rather than by applying labor to them.

But there were too many ahead of him who had the same idea. Although the mineral region of California is as large as the British Isles, he found that these lively brethren had pre-empted every foot of it. He tried Oregon with no better luck, living meanwhile as best he could, by all sorts of expedients —farm work, tramping, storekeeping, peddling—and when he finally went back to his trade, he did it as only another makeshift, for the vision of sudden wealth still haunted him. In a letter to his sister he says that in a dream the night before he was "scooping treasure out of the earth by handfuls, almost delirious with the thoughts of what I would now be able to do, and how happy we would all be"; and he adds wistfully that he supposes he dreamed all this as starving men dream of splendid feasts, or as desert wanderers dream of brooks and fountains.

His trade kept him only very precariously, for times were not easy even then, and there was no great demand for printing or printers. He got a job with one newspaper, then with a second, where, he says, "I worked until my clothes were in rags and the toes of my shoes were out. I slept in the office and did the best I could to economize, but finally I ran in debt thirty dollars for my board bill." He left this job and went adrift again; and then, with no work, no prospects, and with but one piece of money in his pocket, he made a runaway match with a young Australian girl named Annie Fox.

They married not wisely—there is no doubt about that— but wonderfully well, for their marriage appears to have remained perfect until his death in 1897 dissolved it. Balzac called attention to a little-known truth when he said that "a great love is a masterpiece of art," and there are probably about as few really first-rate artists in this field as in any other. Moreover, a masterpiece in this field of art must be a collaboration, and the chance of two first-rate artists finding each other is extremely small, practically a matter of pure luck. A Daphnis in any age may wander over the whole earth without meeting a Chloe, and a Cynthia may survey whole legions of men and never see a Claudius. George's meeting with his wife was almost the only piece of sheer good luck he ever had, but it was a great one. On the night of the twelfth of October, 1883, he wrote this note, and put it by her bedside for her to find next morning:

It is twenty-three years ago tonight since we first met, I only a month or two older than Harry, and you not much older than our Jen. For twenty-three years we have been closer to each other than to anyone else in the world, and I think we esteem each other more and love each other better than when we first began to love. You are now "fat, fair and forty," and to me the mature woman is handsomer and more lovable than the slip of a girl whom twenty-three years ago I met without knowing that my life was to be bound up with hers. We are not rich—so poor just now, in fact, that all I can give you on this anniversary is a little love-letter—but there is no one we can afford to envy, and in each other's love we have what no wealth could compensate for. And so let us go on, true and loving, trusting in Him to carry us farther who has brought us so far with so little to regret.

George kept to his trade, since nothing that looked more lucrative turned up, and after his starving-time of 1864 he began to make a little better living as a printer, though not much better, and he also began to consolidate some sort of position in San Francisco. No sooner was he fairly launched, however, than he threw his future to the winds by enlisting in a filibustering expedition to help out the Mexican patriots who were fighting the French emperor's ill-fated scheme for setting up a vassal empire in Mexico, with the Austrian Archduke Maximilian on the throne. The expedition was a comic-opera affair, planned in a fashion that amounted to piracy, and Providence certainly stood at George's elbow when the Federal authorities put a stop to it before it got under way.

Not satisfied with this grotesque performance, George immediately went into another. He took part in organizing the Monroe League, which was to father a second crusade into Mexico. The league had an elaborate ritual which might have been got up by Gilbert and Sullivan, swearing in its members on a naked sword and the republican flag of Mexico; and Mrs. George, poor soul! was sworn in as the only woman member. One wonders what she really thought of it. The league shortly perished of inanition without having done anything, and George made no further efforts in behalf of the afflicted Mexicans.

These two incidents reveal the one defect in George's natural endowment, which in spite of his superb gifts, his prominence, and his apparent influence over a large and enthusiastic public, made him in the long run ineffectual. He was unquestionably one of the three or four great constructive statesmen of the nineteenth century, perhaps of any century—he ranks with Turgôt. His character was unmatched in the whole public life of his period. He was nobly serious, grandly courageous, and so sincere as to force even his enemies, of whom he had many, to speak well of him. He had great brilliance, some wit, and the command of a fine irony; but he had absolutely no humor. He was as humorless as Oliver Cromwell, a born crusader of the Old Testament type, convinced that he had an Old Testament mission to hew Agag in pieces. All his life he had labored under the unhumorous man's inability to learn what none of us probably enjoys learning, that Truth is a cruel flirt, and must be treated accordingly. Court her abjectly, and she will turn her back; feign indifference, and she will throw herself at you with a coaxing submission. Try to force an acquaintance—try to

make her put on her company manners for a general public
—and she will revolt them like an ugly termagant; let her
take her own way and her own time, and she will show all
her fascinations to every one who has eyes to see them.

IV

George now committed himself to newspaper work, moving from paper to paper in all kinds of capacities, from typesetter to editor and part owner, and by 1868 he had become
prosperous enough to start a bank account. His editorial career was very spirited; he was in one row or another all the
time, and while it may be said that in his treatment of State
and local grievances he was on the popular side, he always
lost. He made things lively for the Associated Press news
monopoly, but though he got an anti-monopoly bill through
the legislature, all that happened was that the monopoly
broke his paper. He fought the Wells-Fargo express monopoly, and lost again—too much money against him. He attacked the Central Pacific's subsidies, and ran for the Assembly as a Democrat on that issue, but again there was too
much money on the other side—the Democrats lost, the
Central Pacific quickly bought up his paper, merged it with
another, and George was out.

So it went. Every turn of public affairs brought up the old
haunting questions. Even here in California he was now seeing symptoms of the same inequality that had oppressed him
in New York. "Bonanza kings" were coming to the front,
and four ex-shopkeepers of Sacramento, Stanford, Crocker,
Huntington, and Hopkins, were laying up immense fortunes
out of the Central Pacific. The railway was bringing in population and commodities, which everybody thought was a
good thing all round, yet wages were going down, exactly as
the old printer in Philadelphia had said, and the masses were
growing worse off instead of better.

About this matter of wages, George had had other testimony besides the old printer's. On his way to Oregon a dozen years before, he fell in with a lot of miners who were talking about the Chinese, and ventured to ask what harm the Chinese were doing as long as they worked only the cheap diggings. "No harm now," one of the miners said, "but wages will not always be as high as they are today in California. As the country grows, as people come in, wages will go down, and some day or other white people will be glad to get those diggings that the Chinamen are working." George said that this idea, coming on top of what the printer had said, made a great impression on him—the idea that "as the country grew in all that we are hoping that it might grow, the condition of those who had to work for their living must become, not better, but worse." Yet in the short space of a dozen years this was precisely what was taking place before his own eyes.

Still, though his two great questions became more and more pressing, he could not answer them. His thought was still inchoate. He went around and around his ultimate answer, like somebody fumbling after something on a table in the dark, often actually touching it without being aware that it was what he was after. Finally it came to him in a burst of true Cromwellian or Pauline drama out of "the commonplace reply of a passing teamster to a commonplace question." One day in 1871 he went for a horseback ride, and as he stopped to rest his horse on a rise overlooking San Francisco Bay—

I asked a passing teamster, for want of something better to say, what land was worth there. He pointed to some cows grazing so far off that they looked like mice, and said, "I don't know exactly, but there is a man over there who will sell some land for a thousand dollars an acre." Like a flash it came over me that there was the reason of advancing poverty with advancing wealth. With the growth of population, land grows in value, and the men who work it must pay more for the privilege.

Yes, there it was. Why had wages suddenly shot up so high in California in 1849 that cooks in the restaurants of San Francisco got $500 a month? The reason now was simple and clear. It was because the placer mines were found on land that did not belong to anybody. Any one could go to them and work them without having to pay an owner for the privilege. If the lands had been owned by somebody, it would have been land-values instead of wages that would have so suddenly shot up.

Exactly this was what had taken place on these grazing lands overlooking San Francisco Bay. The Central Pacific meant to make its terminus at Oakland, the increased population would need the land around Oakland to settle on, and land values had jumped up to a thousand dollars an acre. Naturally, then, George reasoned, the more public improvements there were, the better the transportation facilities, the larger the population, the more industry and commerce—the more of everything that makes for "prosperity"—the more would land values tend to rise, and the more would wages and interest tend to fall.

George rode home thoughtful, translating the teamster's commonplace reply into the technical terms of economics. He reasoned that there are three factors in the production of wealth, and only three: natural resources, labor, and capital. When natural resources are unappropriated, obviously the whole yield of production is divided into wages, which go to labor, and interest, which goes to capital. But when they are appropriated, production has to carry a third charge—rent. Moreover, wages and interest, when there is no rent, are regulated strictly by free competition; but rent is a monopoly-charge, and hence is always "all the traffic will bear."

Well, then, since natural-resource values are purely social

in their origin, created by the community, should not rent go to the community rather than to the individual? Why tax industry and enterprise at all—why not just charge rent? There would be no need to interfere with the private owner-ship of natural resources. Let a man own all of them he can get his hands on, and make as much out of them as he may, untaxed; but let him pay the community their annual rental value, determined simply by what other people would be willing to pay for the use of the same holdings. George could see justification for wages and interest, on the ground of nat-ural right; and for private ownership of natural resources, on the ground of public policy; but he could see none for the private appropriation of economic rent. In his view it was sheer theft. If he was right, then it also followed that as long as economic rent remains unconfiscated, the taxation of in-dustry and enterprise is pure highwaymanry, especially tariff taxation, for this virtually delegates the government's taxing power to private persons.

George worked out these ideas in a tentative way in a forty-eight page pamphlet with the title, "Our Land and Land Policy, National and State," which did not reach many readers, but added something to his reputation as a tribune of the people. The subject mulled in his mind through five years of newspaper work, at the end of which he lost his paper and was once more on the ragged edge. He had begun a maga-zine article on the cause of industrial depressions, but was dissatisfied with it—one could do nothing with the topic in so little space. What was needed was a solid treatise which should recast the whole science of political economy.

He felt that he could write this treatise, but how were he and his family to live meanwhile? He had used his influence on the Democratic side in the last State campaign, and had been particularly instrumental in selecting the governor; so he wrote to Governor Irwin, asking him "to give me a place where there was little to do and something to get, so that I could devote myself to some important writing." The governor gave him the State inspectorship of gas meters, which was a moderately well-paid job, and a sinecure. This was in January, 1876; and in March, 1879, he finished the manuscript of a book entitled *Progress and Poverty; An Inquiry into the Cause of Industrial Depressions, and of Increase of Want with Increase of Wealth; The Remedy.*

V

No one would publish the book, not so much because it was revolutionary (though one firm objected to it emphatically on that ground) but because it was a bad prospect. No work on political economy, aside from textbooks, had ever sold well enough either in the United States or England to make another one attractive. Besides, the unparalleled depression of the 'seventies was making all the publishing houses sail as close to the wind as they could run. Logically, a book on the cause of hard times ought to interest people just then, but book buyers do not buy by logic, and publishers are aware of it.

By hook or crook George and his friends got together enough money to make plates for an author's edition of five hundred copies; George himself set the first few sticks of type. At three dollars a copy he sold enough of these almost to clear the cost; and presently the firm of Appleton, who had rejected the manuscript, wrote him that if he would let them have his plates, they would bring out the book in a two-dollar edition; and this was done.

It fell as dead as Cæsar, not even getting a competent press notice in America for months. George sent some complimentary copies abroad, where it did rather better. Emile de Laveleye praised it highly in the *Revue Scientifique;* it was translated into German, and its reviews, as George said, were *"way* up." Some sort of sale began in March, 1880, with a

brilliant review in *The New York Sun*, which was followed
by more or less serious treatment in the Eastern press generally; but it amounted to almost nothing.

The truth about the subsequent meteoric success of *Progress and Poverty* as a publishing venture is that it was a purely
adventitious success. The times were not only just right for
such a book, but they stayed right for nearly twenty years.
The course of popular interest played directly into its hand,
not only in America, but in the whole English-speaking
world. It is significant that in countries where the course of
interest ran otherwise, as in France, for instance, it had no
vogue. In the English-speaking world, its immense vogue was
almost wholly that of an instrument of discontent, or in the
vernacular of the book trade, a hell-raiser. Even so (to a person who has had any experience at all of the human race),
the fact that a solid treatise like *Progress and Poverty* should
have had an aggregate sale running well over two million
copies is almost incredibly fantastic; yet that is what it had.

From first to last, the history of American civilization is
a most depressing study; but that of the decade from which
Progress and Poverty emerged is probably unmatched in the
whole record, unless by the history of our own times. There
is no need to dwell on it here; one feels utterly degraded at
any reminder of it. George's book nicely caught the tide of
turbulent reaction which brought in "the era of reform" under Cleveland in 1884, and ran fairly full throughout the
'nineties, George's death in 1897 marking the approximate
point of its complete subsidence.

This tidal wave carried George himself as well as his book;
he threw himself on its crest. He expected some good to
come of the great general unrest, and he bent all his energies
to the task of educating the awakened social forces and giving them what he believed to be a right direction. The temper of the times filled him with hope. A sincere republican,
he was a second Jefferson in his naïve idealization of the

common man's intelligence, disinterestedness, and potential loyalty to a great cause. Therefore hell-raising quite suited him; Peter the Hermit had raised hell, and Savonarola had seen no other way to get the common man properly stirred up. Before George was nominated for the mayoralty of New York in 1886, Tammany sent William M. Ivins to buy him off with the promise of a seat in Congress. Ivins told him he could never be mayor—and in fact there is little room for doubt that he was fraudulently counted out—and George asked why, if that were so, there could be any objection to his running. Ivins told him frankly that it was because his running would raise hell; and George replied with similar frankness that that was precisely what he wanted to do.

With this purpose in mind, George came to New York on the heels of his book, selling out what little he possessed in California. "My pleasant little home that I was *so* comfortable in is gone," he wrote sadly, "and I am afloat at forty-two, poorer than at twenty-one. I do not complain, but there is some bitterness in it." During his first year in New York, while his cherished book lay dead, he lived in obscurity, wretchedly poor; and then the time came when he could take advantage of something on which the eyes of the whole English-speaking world were fixed—the Irish rent-war.

VI

Ireland at that time was front-page news on every paper printed in the English language. Parnell and Dillon crossed the ocean, spoke in sixty-two American cities, addressed the House of Representatives, and took away a great fund of American dollars wherewith to fight the battles of the rack-rented Irish tenant. They were followed by the best man in the movement, Michael Davitt, who came over late in 1880 to tend the fire that Parnell and Dillon had kindled. George met him and got him "under conviction," as the revivalists say, and then wrote a pamphlet entitled "The Irish Land Question; what it involves, and how alone it can be settled."

From that moment Henry George was, in the good sense of the term, a made man. The pamphlet was a masterpiece of polemics, a call to action, and a prophecy, all in one. Published simultaneously in America and England, it had an immense success. George was amazed at the space it got in the Eastern papers. "The astonishing thing," he wrote, "is the goodness of the comments. . . . I am getting famous, if I am not making money." It is hard to see how a man who had ever done a day's work on a newspaper could write in that unimaginative way. With Irish influence as strong as it was on the Eastern seaboard, and with every Irishman sitting up nights to curse the hated Sassenach landlords and their puppet government, how could the newspaper comments not be good? The Eastern papers simply knew which side their bread was buttered on.

A rabble of charmed and vociferous Irish closed around the simple-hearted pamphleteer, probably not troubling themselves much about his philosophy of the Irish land question, but nevertheless all for him. He was against the government and against the landlords, and that was enough. In this they were like the vast majority of readers who were led to peck at *Progress and Poverty* because they had heard that the book voiced their discontent; probably not five per cent of them read it through, or were able to understand what they did read, but they were all for it nevertheless, and all for glorifying Henry George. The American branch of the Land League immediately put George on the lecture platform, and when the Irish troubles culminated in the imprisonment of Davitt, Dillon, Parnell, and O'Kelly, an Irish newspaper published in New York sent him to the seat of war as a correspondent.

He reached Dublin, dogged by secret-service men, and gave a public lecture with such effect that his audience went fairly wild. He wrote a friend that he had "the hardest work possible" to keep the crowd from unharnessing his cab-horse and dragging his carriage through the streets to his hotel. His reports to *The Irish World* got wide distribution. When he crossed to England, interest opened many doors to him outside political circles, and curiosity opened many more. He dined with most of the lions of the period, Besant, Herbert Spencer, Tennyson, Justin McCarthy, Wallace, Browning, Chamberlain, John Bright, and made an excellent impression. He wrote his wife that he could easily have become a lion himself if he had liked, but he thought it best to keep clear of all that sort of thing.

He spoke in England, and addressed huge audiences in Scotland. Returning to Ireland, he got still wider publicity out of being locked up twice on suspicion. His notoriety was helped, too, by the humorous character of the proceedings before the examining magistrate, which reminded all England of Mr. Nupkins's examination of the Pickwickians. George took this occasion to write the President a blistering letter about the truckling imbecility of the American Minister, Lowell, and this not only gave him another line of publicity but also had a good practical effect. The Secretary of State sent out a circular letter prodding up the service, and asked George to file a claim for damages, which George refused to do, saying he was not interested in that, but only in seeing that the rights of American citizens in foreign lands were properly defended.

All this celebrity was a great lift for *Progress and Poverty*. The book suddenly became an international best seller. *The London Times* gave it a five-column review which made its fortune in all the British possessions; the review came out in the morning, and by afternoon the publishers had sold out every copy in stock. When a new edition was rushed out, one house in Melbourne ordered 1300 copies, and 300 were sent to New Zealand. George was invited everywhere, banqueted everywhere, asked to speak on all sorts of occasions, reported everywhere; and when he left the British Isles for home, he was perhaps the most widely talked-of man in either hemisphere.

He had intended to stay abroad three months, but remained a year. When he landed in New York he found himself, as he modestly said, "pretty near famous." At once the newspapers blew his horn, the labor unions got up a tremendous mass meeting for him, and, strange as it seems, some of the upper crust of Wall Street gave him a complimentary dinner at Delmonico's, with Justice van Brunt, Henry Ward Beecher, and Francis B. Thurber among the speakers. No one knows why they did this. Possibly it was a more or less perfunctory gesture toward an American who had made a name in England; possibly an inexpensive and non-committal move to please the influential Irish; possibly a gesture of amity toward a man well on his way to becoming a dangerous enemy, but who might be led to see something on their side of social questions. Whatever prompted the occasion, it was a notable affair, and George rose to its measure with easy and affable dignity.

In a sense, this banquet marked the parting of the ways for George, though probably no one was aware of it at the moment, George least of all. A reformer has a choice of three courses. He can carry his doctrine direct to the people, and promote it by methods that are essentially political; he can convert people of power and influence, and promote it largely by indirection; or he can merely formulate it, hang it up in plain sight, and let it win its own way by free acceptance. The first is the course of the evangelists and missionaries; and to a firm believer in eighteenth-century political theory, like George, it is the only one possible—it is wholly republican, wholly in the American tradition. It is interesting to speculate on what might have happened if, for a while at least, he had followed up his one chance to get at the minds of those who really controlled the country's immediate future, or if he had taken the third or Socratic course; but he did neither. He was a stanch republican, committed to republican method.

For the next two years George lived before the populace, speaking and writing incessantly, and directing the development of his doctrine into a distinctly political character. At that time the press was much more an organ of opinion than it is now, much freer and more forceful, so that his writings were in demand. Even a popular publication like *Leslie's* asked him for a series on the problems of the time, while at the other end of the scale *The North American Review* made him a proposal to start a straight-out political and economic weekly under his editorship.

Yet though his method was that of the evangelist, he did not adopt the tactics of the demagog or the practical politician. He was probably the most effective public speaker of his time—*The London Times* thought he was fully the equal of Cobden or of Bright, if not a little better—but he never took advantage of an audience, or flattered the galleries, or left the smallest doubt of where he stood and what was in his mind. When, for example, somebody introduced him in a maudlin way to a working-class audience as "one who was always for the poor man," George began his speech by saying, "Ladies and gentlemen, I am not for the poor man. I am not for the rich man. I am for man."

In fact, it soon became apparent that his hell-raising was raising as much hell with his supporters and potential friends as with his enemies. Like Strafford of old, he was for "thorough," no matter whose head came off or whose toes smarted. All the Irish leaders, even Davitt, cooled off to the freezing point when they found that he was down on the Kilmainham treaty and dead against any compromise on the issues of the rent-war, or any watering down of the program of restoring one hundred per cent of Ireland's land to one hundred per cent of Ireland's people. The Socialists were not unfriendly at first, and some of George's followers thought a sort of working alliance with them might be vamped up for political effect, but when George attacked their doctrine of collectivism and statism, they most naturally showed all their teeth. George held with Paine and Thomas Jefferson that government is at best a necessary evil, and the less of it the better. Hence the right thing was to decentralize it as far as possible, and reduce the functions and powers of the state to an absolute minimum, which, he said, the confiscation of rent would do automatically; whereas the collectivist proposal to confiscate and manage natural resources as a state enterprise would have precisely the opposite effect—it would tend to make the state everything and the individual nothing.

George was moreover the terror of the political routineer. When the Republicans suddenly raised the tariff issue in 1880 the Democratic committee asked him to go on the stump. They arranged a long list of engagements for him, but after he made one speech they begged him by telegraph not to make any more. The nub of his speech was that he had heard of high-tariff Democrats and revenue-tariff Democrats, but he was a no-tariff Democrat who wanted real free trade, and he was out for that or nothing; and naturally no good bipartisan national committee could put up with such talk as that, especially from a man who really meant it.

Yet, on the other hand, when the official free-traders of the Atlantic seaboard, led by Sumner, Godkin, Beecher, Curtis, Lowell, and Hewitt, opened their arms to George, he refused to fall in. His free-trade speeches during Cleveland's second campaign were really devoted to showing by implication that they were a hollow lot, and that their idea of free trade was nothing more or less than a humbug. His speeches hurt Cleveland more than they helped him, and some of George's closest associates split with him at this point. In George's view, freedom of exchange would not benefit the masses of the people a particle unless it were correlated with freedom of production; if it would, how was it that the people of free-trade England, for example, were no better off than the people of protectionist Germany? None of the official free-traders could answer that question, of course, for there was no answer. George had already developed his full doctrine of trade in a book, published in 1886, called *Protection or Free Trade*—a book which, incidentally, gives a reader the best possible introduction to *Progress and Poverty*.

He laid down the law to organized labor in the same style, showing that there was no such thing as a labor-problem, but only a monopoly-problem, and that when natural-resource monopoly disappeared, every question of wages, hours, and conditions of labor would automatically disappear with it. The political liberal got the hardest treatment of all. George seems to have regarded him as the greatest obstruction to social progress—an unsavory compound, half knave, half fool, and flavored odiously with "unctuous rectitude." When John Bright, the Moses of liberalism, followed George on the rostrum at Birmingham, calling his proposals "the greatest, the wildest, the most remarkable . . . imported lately by an American inventor," all George could find to say was (in a private letter) that "the old man is utterly ignorant of what he is talking about"—which was strictly true; and of Frederic Harrison's lectures at Edinburgh and Newcastle he said only that "his is the very craziness of opposition, if I can judge by the reports."

VII

Thus intellectually he was out with every organized force in the whole area of discontent; out with the Socialists, out with the professional Irish, the professional laborites, professional progressivism, liberalism, and mugwumpery. His sympathies and affections however were always with the rank and file of revolt against the existing economic order; his heart was with all the disaffected, though his mind might not be entirely with them. This being so, the two years following his first visit to England fastened upon him the stigma of a mere proletarian class-leader whose principles and intentions were purely predatory. As Abram S. Hewitt most unscrupulously put it, his purpose was no more than "to array working men against millionaires."

Then at the end of these two years there happened the one thing needful to copper-rivet this reputation and make it permanent. When the labor unions of New York City decided to enter the mayoralty campaign of 1886, they looked to George as the best vote-getter in sight, and gave him their nomination. With this, whatever credit he may have had in America as an economist and philosopher vanished forever, leaving him only the uncertain and momentary prestige of a political demagog, an agitator, and a crank.

George had misgivings, not of defeat but of discredit in his rôle of candidate, but they came too late. The course he had chosen years before led straight to the quicksand of practical politics, and now his feet were in it. He temporized with the nomination, demanding a petition signed by thirty thousand citizens pledged to vote for him, which was immediately forthcoming—and there he was!

The campaign was uncommonly bitter. The other candidates were Hewitt and Theodore Roosevelt, and their methods bore hard on George in ways that Hewitt, at any rate, must somewhat have gagged at, for he was a man of breeding—still, he lent himself to them. It was easy to vilify George, because the allegation that he was a sheer proletarian leader was true enough, as far as this campaign went; he was, officially and by nomination, a labor candidate. Some among his supporters, of course, understood his ideas and purposes and believed in them, but these were relatively few; the majority were mere Adullamites. Hewitt won the election nominally—in all reasonable likelihood he was counted in—but George's vote was so large that *The New York Times* saw in it "an event demanding the most serious attention and study"; while *The St. James Gazette*, of London, in a strong grandmotherly vein, advised "all respectable Americans to forget the trumpery of party fights and political differentism, and face the new danger threatening the commonwealth."

As far as George was concerned, there was no need of this warning, for his day in politics was done. This one campaign was the end of him. He was no longer a man to be feared or even reckoned with. To those on the inside of practical politics, he was henceforth hopelessly in the discard as the worst of all liabilities, a defeated candidate. To America at large, he was only another in the innumerable array of bogus prophets and busted spellbinders. Then, too, the temper of the times changed. Disaffection broke up into sects, and popular attention was soon addled by a kaleidoscopic succession of men and issues cleverly manipulated on the public stage—Cleveland and "reform," Hanna and the full dinner-pail, Peffer and populism, McKinley and imperialism, Bryan and free silver, Roosevelt and progressivism; foreign embarrassments, jingoism, the Spanish War, Mrs. Mary Ellen Lease, Mrs. Eddy, Carry Nation, Jerry Simpson, La Follette and the Wisconsin idea, organized charity, "foundations" for this-or-that, the rise of the hire learning, woman's suffrage, the Anti-Saloon League, "commission government" for cities, the initiative and referendum—was ever such a welter of nostrums and nostrum-peddlers turned loose anywhere on earth in the same length of time? No wonder that Mr. Jefferson, mournfully surveying America's prospects, said, "What a Bedlamite is man!" Before a year was over, George had dropped into a historical place amidst all this ruck, from which he has never emerged, as just one more exploded demagog. He ran for a state office in 1887, but got little more than half the votes in New York City, his stronghold, that he had got in the mayoralty campaign only a year before.

The last ten years of his life were devoted largely to a weekly paper, *The Standard*, in which he continued to press his economic doctrine, but it amounted to very little. He revisited England, where he found his former popularity still holding good. He also made a trip around the world, and was received magnificently in his former home, California, and in the British colonies. His main work during this period, however, was writing his *Science of Political Economy*, which his death interrupted; fortunately not until it was so nearly finished that the rest of his design for it could be easily filled in.

In this period, too, his circumstances, for the first time in his life, were fairly easy. He had received some small gifts and legacies, and latterly a couple of well-to-do friends saw to it that he should finish his work without anxiety. It is an interesting fact that George stands alone in American history as a writer whose books sold by the million, and as an orator whose speech attracted thousands, yet who never made a dollar out of either.

His death had a setting of great drama or of great pathos, according to the view that one chooses to take of it. The municipal monstrosity called the Greater New York was put together in the late 'nineties, and some of George's friends and associates, still incorrigibly politically minded, urged on him the forlorn hope of running as an independent candidate for the mayoralty in 1897. Seth Low, then president of Columbia University, and Robert van Wyck, who was the impregnable Tammany's candidate, were in the field—the outcome was clear—yet George acceded. It is incredible that he could have had the faintest hope of winning; most probably he thought it would be one more chance, almost certainly his last, to bear testimony before the people of his adopted city with the living voice.

He had had a touch of aphasia in 1890, revealing a weakness of the blood vessels in his brain, and his condition now was such that every physician he consulted told him he could not possibly stand the strain of a campaign; and so it proved. He opened his campaign at a rapid pace, speaking at one or more meetings every night, nearly always with all his old clearness and force. Three weeks before election he spoke at four meetings in one evening, and went to bed at the Union Square Hotel, much exhausted. Early next morning his wife awoke to find him in an adjoining room, standing in the attitude of an orator, his hand on the back of a chair, his head erect and his eyes open. He repeated the one word "yes" many times, with varying inflections, but on becoming silent he never spoke again. Mrs. George put her arm about him, led him back to his bed with some difficulty, and there he died.

VIII

Progress and Poverty is the first and only thorough, complete, scientific inquiry ever made into the fundamental cause of industrial depressions and involuntary poverty. The ablest minds of the century attacked and condemned it—Professor Huxley, the Duke of Argyll, Goldwin Smith, Leo XIII, Frederic Harrison, John Bright, Joseph Chamberlain. Nevertheless, in a preface to the definitive edition, George said what very few authors of a technical work have ever been able to say, that he had not met with a single criticism or objection that was not fully anticipated and answered in the book itself. For years he debated its basic positions with any one who cared to try, and was never worsted.

Yet, curiously, though there have been a number of industrial depressions since George's death in 1897, some of them very severe, the book has been so completely obscured by the reputation which George's propagandist enterprises fastened on him, that one would not know it had been written. In the whole course of the recent depression, for instance, no utterance of any man at all prominent in our public life, with one exception, would show that he had ever heard of it. The president of Columbia University resurrected George in a commencement address two years ago, and praised him warmly, but from what he said he seems not to have read him.

It is interesting, too, now that successive depressions are bearing harder and harder on the capitalist, precisely as George predicted, to observe that George and his associate anti-monopolists of forty years ago are turning out to be the best friends that the capitalist ever had. Standing stanchly for the rights of capital, as against collectivist proposals to confiscate interest as well as rent, George formulated a defense of those rights that is irrefragable. All those who have tried to bite that file have merely broken their teeth. There is a certain irony in the fact that the class which has now begun to suffer acutely from the recurring prostrations of industry and the ever-growing cost of stateism, is the very one which assailed George most furiously as an "apostle of anarchy and revolution." Yet the rapid progress of collectivism and stateism could have been foreseen; there was every sign of it, and the capitalist class should have been the one to heed those signs devoutly and interpret them intelligently. Bismarck saw what was coming, and even Herbert Spencer predicted terrible times ahead for England, and still more terrible times for America—a long run of statism and collectivism, then "civil war, immense bloodshed, ending in a military despotism of the severest type."

IX

Like John Bright, nearly every one credited the "American inventor" with a brand-new discovery in his idea of confiscating economic rent. George did in fact come by the idea independently, but others whom he had never heard of came by it long before him. Precisely the same proposal had been made in the eighteenth century by men whom Mr. Bright might have thought twice about snubbing—the French school known as the Economists, which included Quesnay, Turgôt, du Pont de Nemours, Mirabeau, le Trosne, Gournay. They even used the term *l'impôt unique*, "the single tax," which George's American disciples arrived at independently, and which George accepted. The idea of confiscating rent also occurred to Patrick Edward Dove at almost the same time that it occurred to George. It had been broached in England almost a century earlier by Thomas Spence, and again in Scotland by William Ogilvie, a professor at Aberdeen. George's doctrine of the confiscation of social values was also explicitly anticipated by Thomas Paine, in his pamphlet called *Agrarian Justice.*

George's especial merit is not that of original discovery, though his discovery was original—as much so as those of Darwin and Wallace. It was simply not new; Turgôt had even set forth the principle on which George formulated the law of wages, though George did not know that any one had done so. George's great merit is that of having worked out his discovery to its full logical length in a complete system, which none of his predecessors did; not only establishing fundamental economics as a true science, but also discerning and clearly marking out its natural relations with history, politics, and ethics.

The key to an understanding of George's career may be found in the story that Lincoln Steffens tells about an afternoon ride with the devil on the top of a Fifth Avenue bus. The devil was in uncommonly good spirits that day, and entertained Steffens with a fine salty line of reminiscences half way up the avenue, when Steffens suddenly caught sight of a man on the sidewalk who was carefully carrying a small parcel of truth. Steffens nudged the devil, who gave the man a casual glance, but kept on talking, apparently not interested. When Steffens could get a word in, he said, "See here, didn't you notice that that man back there had got hold of a little bit of truth?"

"Yes, of course I noticed it," replied the devil. "Why?"

"But surely that's a very dangerous thing," Steffens said. "Aren't you going to do something about it?"

"No hurry, my dear fellow," the devil answered indulgently. "It's a simple matter. I'll be running across him again one of these days, and I'll get him to organize it!"

It is impossible, of course, to guess what George's historical position would now be if he had had less of the Covenanter spirit and more of the experienced and penetrating humor of a Socrates, with a corresponding distrust of republican method in the propagation of doctrine. The question is an idle one, yet to a student of civilization the great interest of George's career is that at every step he makes one ask it. Perhaps in any case the Gadarene rout would have trampled him to the same depth of obscurity. Probably—almost certainly—his doctrine would have been picked up and wrested to the same service of a sectarian class-politics that would have left it unrecognizable. Experience, humor, and reason go for very little when they collide with what Ernest Renan so finely called *la matérialisme vulgaire, la bassesse de l'homme intéressé.* Yet one can hardly doubt that George would emerge from obscurity sooner, and his doctrine stand in a clearer and more favorable light if he had taken another course.

Much more important, however, is the question whether George's faith in the common man's collective judgment was justified; whether such faith is ever justified. Does the common man possess the force of intellect to apprehend the processes of reason correctly, or the force of character to follow them disinterestedly? The whole future of eighteenth-century political doctrine, the doctrine on which our republic was nominally established, hangs on this question—the question, in short, whether republicanism has not put a burden on the common man which is greater than he can bear.

George never had a moment's doubt of the answer. Yet, seeing what sort of political leadership the common man invariably chose to follow, and the kind of issue that invariably attracted him, he ended the argument of *Progress and Poverty* with a clear warning, too long to be quoted here, against the wholesale corruption of the common man by the government which the common man himself sets up. It is well worth reading now, whether one finds the root of this corruption in the common man's weakness of mind and character, or whether one finds it, as George did, in the unequal distribution of wealth. Whatever one may think about that, there is no possible doubt that George's warning has the interest of absolutely accurate prophecy.

It is rather remarkable, finally, since the reading public's whim for biography has set writers to pawing over so many American worthies, that no one has written a competent full-length biography of Henry George, who was not only one of America's very greatest men, but also was in so many respects typically American, and whose spectacular career was also so typical. His disabilities were precisely those of the civilization that produced him, and his life was sacrificed on the altar of those disabilities, precisely where the life of that civilization is being sacrificed. What more by way of interest could an able and honest biographer ask?

WHAT THE AMERICAN VOTES FOR

My first and only presidential vote was cast many, many years ago. It was dictated by pure instinct. I remember the circumstances well. Like all well-brought-up youngsters, I had been told that it was the duty of every citizen to vote—reasons not stated. I was prepared to obey in all good faith, and accordingly, when the time came, I set forth to the polls.

But what was I to vote for? An issue? There was none. You could not get a sheet of cigarette-paper between the official positions of the two parties. A candidate? Well, who were they? Both of them seemed to me to be mediocre time-serving fellows who would sell out their immortal souls, if they had any, for a turn at place and power, and throw in their risen Lord for good measure. Suddenly, the ridiculous truth of the matter struck me: that the whole campaign was based on no political reason at all, but on an astronomical reason. We were voting simply because, since the time we last voted, the earth had gone 1461 times around the sun, or some such number, and for no other reason in the world. As I approached the polls my resentment of this nonsense grew stronger and stronger, and when I arrived I deliberately wrote in a vote for Jefferson Davis of Mississippi.

It was not an ignorant vote, for I was fully aware that Jeff was dead. Nor was it a piece of mere flippancy—far from it. I found out afterward that either Mark Twain or Artemus Ward, I forget which, had once done something of the kind, on the plea that "if we can't have a live statesman, let us by all means have a first-class corpse." There is a great deal to be said for that idea, and I am proud to subscribe to it, but it was not my idea at the time. My vote was a vote of serious protest against what I regarded as an impudent and degrading absurdity, and at this late day I am more than ever prepared to maintain that the instinct which prompted it was sound and enlightened. I am also prepared to show cause for believing that this instinct actually controls the majority of our electorate, whether they are aware of it or not, and to show cause for believing that they are fully justified in letting it control them.

Visiting Englishry, especially English politicians, are usually struck by what they call the American's lack of interest in politics. We seem to them to have no sense of personal concern with national affairs—that is, of course, the majority of us, exclusive of those who have something at stake, like a tariff-schedule, or something in the way of jobhunting, subsidy or graft. The last one I remember as speaking about this was Miss Margaret Bondfield, who was a member of the late Labor Cabinet. She used our Sunday press to read us a good schoolmarm's lecture on the subject, and there is no denying that she brought in a true bill.

As these English visitors see it, the American's interest in politics (provided he has no ax to grind) differs from the Englishman's in being occasional, not continuous. It is a sporting interest, like interest in a horse-race. When election-day is over, he forgets it, buckles down to his job, and contentedly leaves Washington to the mercy of such lobbyists, crooks, blacklegs, editors, politicians and desperadoes as normally find their way there, seeking what they may devour.

These foreign visitors also say that the American's interest differs from the Englishman's in being more concerned with men than with issues. They account for this by the fact that the official issues of our national campaigns are so trivial that they are really no issues at all, and that therefore the actual cleavage between our parties is not spacious. In other words, we have nothing that an Englishman would understand by an effective political Opposition. Hence whatever public interest there may be in an election must focus on the personality of the candidates.

There can be no doubt, I repeat, that this is a true bill. It takes a heroic deal of prodding to goad the free-born American sovereign into wielding his royal prerogative on election day. An immense amount of money and energy is spent on getting out the vote, but the result is never impressive. If 40% of the total electorate turns out and votes, it is a good haul, and 50% is a large one. If local contests did not coincide with national contests, the national vote would be even slimmer than it is.

I shall not take up space to fortify Miss Bondfield's true bill by discussing the official issues of the last campaign, or the width of the cleavage between the two parties. Nothing of all this impressed me particularly, but that is a small matter. I do not think it would have made much more of an impression on the average Frenchman or Englishman, but that need not be considered, either. Beyond doubt, however, the personality of the candidates, or of one candidate, counted for a great deal. It was actually, though not officially, the major issue. A very large proportion of the vote was cast in complete disregard of any question, except that of pure personal sentiment, favorable or unfavorable, towards Mr. Hoover.

As for the post-election lapse of interest which now, once more, mystifies foreign observers, I see nothing mysterious about it. All those who have an ax to grind are of course very busy—job-seekers, bankers, brewers, farmers, railroad men, everyone who stands to gain or lose something. Aside from these, now that the sporting event is over, the general run of the electorate has resumed its customary attitude of profound detachment. As far as it keeps any track at all of national affairs, it views them as a spectator and not as a participant. It waits to "see what they'll do" and makes more or less idle conjectures, shaped largely by the journalists, on what it will be. But, as usual, there is little if any personal concern with "their" doings or misdoings.

II

Now, what about this attitude? Does it prove that the American is politically ignorant, shiftless, irresponsible, and gets no better government than he deserves? I say no. All that may be true—in fact, I think it *is* true—but his attitude towards national politics does not prove it. Moreover, if he be ignorant and undeserving, it is fair to point out that his political institutions give him no incentive to be less so. Furthermore, if he were ever so informed and ever so interested and lively, his institutions give him no adequate means of making his will effective. "American efficiency," as expressed in American political institutions, certainly means the poorest, slowest, most discouraging and incompetent way of getting anything done.

In the many long years that have elapsed since my one and only presidential vote was cast, I have seen an enormous amount of blame and obloquy shovelled on the nape of the American sovereign for his attitude of detachment. I can speak of this with a certain degree of personal concern, because it has been shovelled on me, I being that American sovereign—one of them—and that attitude being mine. I have waited a long time for some abler person to come out and defend it, but nobody has done so, and I therefore undertake to defend it myself. In so doing I may say that for once in my life, perhaps the only time, I have the pleasing consciousness that I am speaking for many millions of my fellow-sovereigns.

We are blamed for laziness, triviality, carelessness, lack of patriotism. If public affairs are ever in a bad way, it is our fault. If we do not express our will at the polls, and do not strive between elections to have it carried out, what may we expect but a reign of corruption, oppression and bureaucracy? Not long ago our fine old friend, Mr. Wickersham, got into such a pucker over our shortcomings that he proposed some scheme of compulsory voting, under penalty, as I recall it, of fine or jail—good sound paternalistic doctrine! Every once in a while somebody publishes a magazine article urging us to take more interest in politics. I remember that the new Governor of New York, Mr. Lehman, published one lately that was very fine and striking. And all sorts of clubs and societies are on foot to educate the apathetic electorate and stir it into action.

If the rest of our delinquent sovereigns feel as I do, I may say that we do not particularly resent these efforts. We are inclined to be rather meek under the odium that is put on us. Mr. Wickersham's idea, now, is perhaps another matter; we might think that would be crowding the mourners a little. But in general we are willing to be patient and reasonable, for we are not so ignorant and stupid as we may appear to be, and we really would like, as much as anybody, to have things go ship-shape and happily. All we ask is that our monitors should be a little patient and reasonable too, and listen to us fairly while we make a very simple plea of extenuating circumstances.

Let us look at the last election. Millions of voters got four years worth of bile out of their systems on election day, and were more chipper and cheerful next morning than they had been for months. This was all to the good, no doubt, but the benefit seems rather in the scope of pathology than in that of politics. A large majority registered their opinion that Mr. Hoover was not a satisfactory public servant, and this also was all very well. But if that is the way we felt towards Mr.

Hoover, why should we have had to put up with him for four years before dismissing him?

The French or English can turn out an unsatisfactory public servant at any time. They do not have to wait four years; they can do it in four hours. They have the political machinery for doing that, and we have not; if we had, Mr. Hoover would probably have gone out of office at least two years and a half ago. My point is that people who have no machinery for making their political will immediately effective cannot reasonably be expected to take much interest in a mere hopeful registration of what they want.

The "will of the people" repudiated Republican rule last November, with almost unprecedented emphasis. Why do we have to wait four months before it can really count? In England or France it would get action at once, almost in four minutes. When an English or French government is hit by a vote of no confidence, out it goes on the spot, and the party or combination that has ousted it goes in. We all remember the series of French governments a couple of years ago that one after another went down like a row of dominoes, almost before the members took their seats. One of our newspaper paragraphers said at the time that the French Premiership was one turn around in a revolving door. It was commonly understood, though I do not know how true it was, that an international conference had to be postponed until the French found a Premier who could hold his job long enough to make the trip from Paris to London and back before he was fired out.

In the last election we voted against Mr. Hoover—that is plain enough—but what did we vote *for?* Many, presumably, voted for beer; all right, we will find no fault with that. On the contrary, let us assume that the whole prodigious majority voted for beer. But all it got was a vague promise of beer on some uncertain tomorrow. The English have governmental machinery whereby if they vote for beer they get it at once, and without going through any further motions. If the people say beer, they pass the word to the House of Commons, and when the House says beer, beer it is, and that is the end of the matter.

If, by some trick of the politicians, we get only bad beer, or prohibitively costly beer, or no beer at all, there is nothing we can do about it but wait until the end of another "fixed term." Suppose Mr. Roosevelt and his crew find it to their political or personal advantage not to give us a lower tariff, or whatever we all may in good faith have voted for (and this has often happened, e.g., the great tariff-betrayal in 1894, and the war-betrayal under Wilson, who got his second term because "he kept us out of war"), what can we do about it, short of another four years? Nothing. And what kind of executive usurpations, indignities and rascalities does our history show may be practiced on us with impunity meanwhile?

The fixed term means simply that ours is not a representative government at all, but a delegated government. The vote that seats our President, our Congress, our State and municipal officials, is simply a *carte blanche*, or rather, something in the nature of a letter-of-marque. How can an intelligent citizen be expected to take interest in the conduct of politics under these conditions?

Even if our elected officials all stand by us loyally, we cannot get what we vote for except on the sufferance of nine old men, irresponsible, inaccessible, appointed for life, and concerning whose appointment the people have nothing to say. The intelligent citizen knows this, knows that even with the President and Congress unanimously on his side, his actual sovereignty amounts to exactly nothing. The Supreme Court is the actual sovereign power, the final law-making authority—not law-interpreting, but law-making. How, then, can the citizen be interested? What the British House of Commons says goes, even for the King on his throne, and it goes straight off the bat; the Britisher knows it, and he feels and acts accordingly.

Moreover, not only can the American citizen do nothing between elections to make his will effective, or to bring retribution on those who thwart it, but his party can do nothing. The thing that most keeps the Englishman's interest in politics alive between elections is the power of the Opposition; and the power of the Opposition lies in the fact that it can turn out the government at any moment when it can command a majority in the House. "His Majesty's loyal Opposition" sits in the House like a cat by a rat-hole, waiting for the government to make a break on some question, small or large, that will shift enough sentiment to pass a vote of no confidence —and then, down goes the government. No one can tell when this may happen, and the constant surveillance of the Opposition tends to make the government prayerfully watch its step.

This sort of machinery makes any change possible and practicable at any time the people want it. If the government is fairly sure that the people do not want the change, it can always "go to the country"—that is, hold an election on *that issue*. The issue is likely to be a pretty real one, and thus it is that the British voter gets the habit of regarding politics as a matter of issues rather than of men.

III

Again, how can the American voter be expected to have any interest in the doings of the Executive between elections, when the whole Executive is irresponsible and ungetatable by any means short of a congressional investigation, which takes dynamite to start, and is a matter of months spent in all sorts of futile and vexatious foolery?

The President picks his Cabinet where he likes, and they

are utterly inaccessible; they cannot be seen or spoken to unless they choose, let alone called to account. The British Prime Minister must choose his Cabinet from the House, and they keep their seats in the House and can be called to account by any member. Once when I was in London a member got up at question-time, took an envelope out of his pocket, and said, "Mr. Speaker, I wish to ask the Postmaster-General," who was sitting about fifteen feet in front of him, "why he did not deliver this letter on time." The letter belonged to some constituent who had kicked about it to his representative, and got him to put the question. The Postmaster-General asked for time to look the matter up, and in a few days made his reply, and the thing was properly straightened out. He had to do that, or he would have lost his job.

That is the British equivalent of a congressional investigation, whether concerning a small matter like a delayed letter, or a large matter like a profiteering army contract. It is direct, simple, business-like. There you have the machinery of really representative and responsible government. The citizen who has that kind of machinery at his disposal can afford to be interested in politics because he knows he can get action and get it at once.

It is even conceivable that the government might have fallen on the apparently petty occasion of that delayed letter. Such a thing has happened, and it could happen again. Suppose the government has only a small majority and is not very popular; suppose the Opposition has smelt out a few disaffected votes that they think may turn the scale; suppose the Postmaster-General is evasive and does not give a straight answer. The leader of the Opposition makes a red-hot speech, asking Mr. Speaker what in Heaven's name he thinks the Empire is coming to, when a venal and bungling government won't let His Majesty's loyal subjects get their mail. Some one on the government bench, perhaps the Prime Minister, replies as best he can—then a vote of "no confidence," and down goes the government.

I was once told in London that one government had just missed destruction by the closest kind of shave, on what would seem to us the curious issue of a girl having been picked up by the police for soliciting. She told the police that she was a daughter of the rector of some church out in the country, that she had lost her direction on Piccadilly, and had stopped a stranger to ask her way. The police detained her overnight. Next day it turned out that she *was* that rector's daughter, and that her story was true.

At question-time that afternoon, the member for her district was on his feet with fire in his eye, asking the Home Secretary what in high hell he meant by sloughing up the daughter of his rector, and the government was in a hole, knowing that every newspaper in the Kingdom would be on the warpath next morning. As I got the story, the government compounded handsomely within two hours, with an apology and a cash indemnity, and so saved its neck.

I pass by the Electoral College, that remarkable institution which every once in a while gives us a minority President, like Harrison. Why should any one who voted in that election, when Cleveland got the votes and Harrison got the Presidency, ever take the trouble to vote again, at least until the Electoral College is abolished and the President elected by direct vote? I see no reason why he should do so.

Finally, how can we be interested in politics when our Constitution makes the existence of a national issue impossible? The provision which obliges our representatives to reside in their districts automatically converts every issue into a local issue. We have at last learned that General Hancock told the truth—which so mystified the country at the time —when he said that the tariff is a local issue. But so is every issue, and must be; Prohibition, for instance, is notoriously a local issue. What is one to think, really, of the state of politics where the Constitution forbids the legislature to take any but a purely parochial view of every public question?

The United States is often criticized for having no continuous foreign policy. But this provision of the Constitution makes it impossible to have any foreign policy at all. The members of the Foreign Relations committees of Senate and House must live in their districts, and each one must first and foremost reflect the prevailing interests and sentiment of his district, or lose his job. He simply cannot afford to take a national view of any foreign relation, even if he were ever so willing and able to do so. He may take a national view only in so far as it is not incompatible with local interest.[1] Hence every change in the personnel of these committees brings new sets of local interests to the fore, and our policy is merely a series of improvisations.

In England, on the other hand, a representative who falls out with his constituents over a matter of public policy may get himself put up in any other district in the whole Kingdom where he thinks local sentiment will support him. He may be an utter stranger who has never set foot in that district in his life, but that does not matter. If we had that mechanism, a dry Rhode Island Congressman, for instance, could go out and put himself up for some safe dry district in Maine or Kansas. A pacifist devotee of the League of Nations, living in an armament-making district of Pennsylvania, could get himself put up in some mid-Western district where sentiment ran the other way. This mechanism, obviously, tends to preserve dignity, integrity, self-respect, all round. If we had it we need not have been disgraced by the odious spectacle of the dry-voting, wet-drinking legislator; nor by the more odious spectacle of the rush for the band-wagon.

[1] Those who feel inclined to doubt this may be referred to the disgraceful history of the dispute with Canada over the fisheries question, in Cleveland's first administration. Examples are plentiful enough, but this one will suffice.

IV

Nevertheless, Mr. Wickersham might say, it all comes back to the people in the end. If our institutions seem expressly designed—as every one who knows their history knows they were designed—to paralyze our activity and suffocate our interest, why do the people put up with them? Why are we not whooping for reform? Why not unite, organize, get up "campaigns of education" and all that sort of thing, in the orthodox American way, and crusade for a brand-new set of political machinery?

This is plausible. It has the right sound, and is all right "in principle," as the diplomats say, but it is actually impracticable. We have seen those crusades before, and we know what happens to them when they meet what Ernest Renan so finely calls *la bassesse de l'homme interessé*. Suppose the Forgotten Man, who is about 80% of our population, asked Mr. Roosevelt and his horde of voracious Democrats to pause on their way to the trough long enough to call a constitutional convention aimed at the reforms I have suggested. Would they do it? Not in the whole history of our republican institutions is there a single incident to warrant the suspicion that they would. But suppose they did, then that same history enables us to forecast exactly what sort of convention we would get. We can see the whole make-up of it in our mind's eye; it would be made up of the very people who have every interest in keeping our political machinery exactly as it is.

No, there is nothing in crusading. The English can have what the Duke of Wellington called "a revolution by due course of law" whenever they think the occasion warrants it. They have the machinery for doing it, and we have not. There remains to us only the recourse to violence, which is no doubt our privilege, but is not to be considered, for we have no confidence in it. Probably our descendents will have to come to something of the kind, but it is nothing for us at the moment. We have learned something from our own revolutions and also from those in other lands; the outcome would be far too uncertain.

It turns out, then, that our practical instinct about politics is sound. All that the Forgotten Man can do is what we so largely find him doing. He can take our national politics as supplying him with a recurrent sporting event, a sort of extravaganza, in which the actors appear to him as more or less clever mountebanks, and his own relation to it is that of a spectator who is only mildly stirred. He may walk out on it, and usually does so whenever anything more attractive comes along; that is to say, as a rule, when he is not wholly idle. He may use it as an occasion for the display of resentment; indeed, the returns seem generally to show that this is the most nearly serious use he ever makes of it. To expect more than this of him seems to me unreasonable, whatever Mr. Wickersham may say; and whether more be expected of him or not, this appears to be about all he will do.

BRET HARTE AS A PARODIST

With a Note on Nationalism in Literature

IN GENERAL, probably, when all considerations are duly balanced, it may be said that nationalism is a bad thing for literature. When a nation becomes "great"—that is, when it begins to cut a big figure in industry and trade—it usually begins to feel that it must have a great art to match. It must have a great literature, great poetry, great music, great painting. If it has not already got them it must either valiantly pretend that what it has got is great or else bend its energies to a mechanical sort of improvisation in greatness. For example, in the last century, when Germany became a great world power in the political and economic sense, she felt the imperious need of a great literature; and (apart from scientific and philosophic literature) not having it, she set to work resolutely to glorify what she had and made a rather unconvincing job of it. To the mind unprepossessed by German nationalism, German literature, with the exceptions noted, has not been successfully recommended by the nationalist appraisal. A single illustration will suffice. In her rapid progress towards industrial, commercial and political eminence, Germany felt the appropriateness of having an eminent epic poem to correspond; so she took the *Nibelungenlied*, inflated her own critical estimate of it considerably, and put it before the attention of the rest of the world. She already possessed great music, music universally acknowledged as of the very first order; and her music in the person of Richard Wagner went out to service of the nationalist spirit in the bolstering up and exploitation of the *Nibelungenlied* as one of the world's great epics. Even with the aid of this powerful auxiliary, the attempt failed. The world did not accept Germany's critical estimate even when that estimate bore the stamp of this adventitious, but highly persuasive, recommendation. It remained fully appreciative, fully disposed to give generous credit and admiration where they were due—no one can pretend that it did not—but fully aware that the *Nibelungenlied* is not a great epic poem, and that no effort of nationalist imagination can make it so. Even at that, the world's judgment was happy to make a differentiation in favor of a certain temperamental partiality, as when someone told a French critic that Béranger was not really a great poet, and the Frenchman replied, "True, he is not; but *for us*, he is." Nothing can be said against the legitimacy and soundness of this view; but the nationalist spirit is usually not content to regard the matter in this objective fashion. It is dissatisfied with anything short of a general consent to the validity of its own estimate.

The nationalist spirit in the United States took an opposite course. When we became a world power, in the modern sense, and began to feel the appropriateness of having a great literature to correspond, our tendency was rather to slight the merits of such literature as we already had, and to magnify the prospects of what we were going to produce. The tacit assumption of our nationalism was that the great American novel, drama, poem, had not yet been written, but that we were "going strong," very strong indeed, and that at any moment now they might be expected. In fact, every publisher was sure he had them already on the press, and felt no false modesty about proclaiming his certainty; while reviewers took their cue from publishers and backed up their pretensions with columns of resonant and stereotyped fustian. So far did all this extravagance go, as we are all aware, that book reviewing largely passed over from its own legitimate field into that of a kind of brummagem criticism. It developed an abominable glossary of its own by wresting to a special use such words as *intrigue, derive, arresting, vibrant, vital*—we all know them; and the joint efforts of reviewer and publisher even made necessary the coinage of the special descriptive word, "blurb."

In short, in our manifestation of the nationalist spirit as compared, say, with Germany's, we are "forward-looking," and there is, of course, some virtue in that. It is a hopeful attitude, and hopefulness is exhilarating. It is a hospitable attitude, and hospitality is meritorious. Yet one may frankly doubt but what our course has been the worse for literature. After all, to go back to our illustration, the *Nibelungenlied* was, for the German, at least a fixed quantity, it was *there*, and considerable time had passed over its head. It was therefore possible for a German to put a deliberate discount on his nationalism, to take a disinterested view of his epic, and appraise it accordingly. He could do this, moreover, undistracted by the haunting uncertainty that seems to beset criticism when exercised under the influence of a forward-looking nationalism—the fear of taking *omne novum pro magnifico*, whether for better or for worse. Our type of nationalism keeps criticism sitting on the edge of the chair in impatience for the advent of something, it knows not what; and keeps it meanwhile continuously discomposed and dishevelled by a thunderous succession of false alarms.

In view of this, it has often occurred to me that serious criticism in this country would do well resolutely to break with our nationalism, and devote itself to re-appraising the literature produced, let us say, up to twenty years ago. It is at least debatable whether criticism has ever any proper business with contemporary literature. Goethe, the greatest of critics, thought not. "Don't read your fellow-strivers, fellow-workers," was his uncompromising word on the subject. It is noticeable, too, that other great critics show an instinct for going at contemporary literature with very long teeth. They seem instinctively to prefer letting time sift it a little before they take it up. Emerson's observation on this—"never read a book until it is at least a year old"—is well known, and it has the merit of sterling good sense in any circumstances; but in circumstances like ours, with the nationalist spirit marshalling us so rigorously the other way, it deserves unquestioning acceptance. By so doing, our criticism may rehabilitate itself and become respectable, and again it may not; but otherwise it surely never can. Serious criticism need not fear that our nationalism will go begging if deprived of its support. There will still be plenty of blurbs, plenty of the journalistic treatment of literature, plenty of forward-looking reviewers, plenty of literary log-rolling. Nationalism can very handily do without the serious critic's co-operation; and meanwhile the serious critic can devote himself undisturbed to the revamping and rehabilitation of his legitimate business which has long been in so bad a way as to be almost no business at all.

I have even thought that a literary publication might make a good feature out of some straight reviews of old books, reviews that should relate these books as strictly to the present as if they had just come off the press. This notion came up in my mind again the other day when I was re-reading Turgenev's *Fathers and Children* and remarking its apparent applicability to the spiritual circumstances of modern Russia, as far as I understand them. I should think that a critical review of that book would interest a reflective Russian considerably. For my own part, I should greatly like to read a straight group-review of John Hay's *Breadwinners*, Henry Adams's *Democracy* and Warner-Clemens's *The Gilded Age*. In another field, a competent reviewer could do something interesting with Ignatius Donnelly's *Atlantis*. In yet another, with Henry George's *Protection or Free Trade*. I am postulating,

I repeat, that this reviewing should all be done from the standpoint of our own actual present circumstances, political, intellectual, social, spiritual, quite as if they were brand-new books by authors previously unknown. Similarly, in still another field, I should like to read an essay which should be not quite so much a group-review as a critical group-study of four minor—very minor—literary men of the last century, a study which should address itself to one question: i.e., how is it that the literary ability of R. W. Gilder, E. S. Nadal, Charles DeKay and Maurice Francis Egan never came to more than it did? I can imagine the country-wide chorus of Homeric laughter that this question would raise if it were put to our professors of English literature, but on the other hand I can imagine a disinterested and capable critic looking into it and finding that it led him a long way in unsuspected directions and through a survey of unlooked-for fields.

A really fresh, unprepossessed eye turned back on the body of our literature for the sake of what it might find there, and not for purposes of nationalist exploitation or of fastening on something and giving it a spectacular run of revival, as in the case of Melville a few years ago, might succeed in turning up some matters of fairly conspicuous literary merit. For instance, it might be shown, I think, and shown to a very good and useful purpose, that our literature contains about the best parody ever written. I do not remember ever having seen the name of Bret Harte brought forward in this connection; it no doubt has been, but I think not regularly. Matthew Arnold remarked that parody is a vile art, as it may be, but he gave it full credit for being an art, as it undoubtedly is; and there is an advantage in knowing where uncommonly good specimens of any are to be found. It is with this advantage only, and not with shifting the incidence of nationalism, that criticism is concerned. Our interest is only in knowing where to get at the best specimens of an art, and one very bad effect of nationalism is, as in this case, that it stands in the way of this knowledge. A sound literary interest is not in Harte as an American or even as a parodist, but in parody as an art, and in the fact that the best examples of it are to be found in one place rather than another; and the business of criticism is to keep open an access to these examples, to show wherein their merit lies and what their practical uses are. Further, when this access is blocked by the interference of anything alien to a purely literary interest, such as the nationalist spirit, it is the business of criticism to take up arms against the encroachment.

In 1870 Harte wrote a thin little volume called *Condensed Novels*, made up of seventeen parodies of authors current at the time. The book got some popularity, enough to move him to try his hand at a second series which for a reason that I shall presently mention did not do so well as the first. A critic need not trouble himself with the second series; it is not particularly good; but the first series repays careful attention. I shall not offer a critical study of it here, for my point is not so much the establishment of Harte's place in literature, as the consideration of parody as an art and of Harte's claims as an artist. My point is rather to arouse the critic to the insidious influence of the nationalist spirit in keeping us so steadily looking forward that we lose track of past achievements which even nationalism itself might very well use for its own purposes. Nationalism's loss is of course not important; the important thing is that we all lose the benefit of a significant achievement by having our access to it virtually cut off, and that criticism should be prompt in showing where and what the interference is, and in doing all it can to restore our access.

Harte's superiority as a parodist lies, first, in the sound literary instinct that led him to choose great subjects for his parodies. I am speaking, and shall speak throughout, only of his first series. His second series failed because he ran out of great subjects, and tried to make shift with subjects that were really too slight for effective parody. Fifteen out of his seventeen subjects in the first series were the most eminent popular writers of his period: Dickens, Charlotte Brontë, Reade, Wilkie Collins, Disraeli, Lever, Bulwer-Lytton, Marryat and the author of *Guy Livingstone* were the British representatives; also an imaginary Braddon-Wood collaboration. France gave him Hugo and Dumas, and the United States gave him Cooper. Two of his subjects were not great literary figures by any means, but they were conspicuously associated with great social and political circumstances, and thus became themselves conspicuous, so Harte's instinct in choosing them still remained a sound one. Belle Boyd was a notable spy of the Confederacy, and her memoirs lent themselves well to parody, especially as they gave occasion for an incidental playful drive at the pachydermatous British journalist, G. A. Sala, against whom Matthew Arnold loosed such exquisite raillery in *Friendship's Garland*. T. S. Arthur was the old, original anti-saloon, anti-liquor, total-abstinence propagandist. He may, I think, be called the godfather of the movement which has culminated in the Eighteenth Amendment and the Volstead Act. One of his books, *Ten Nights in a Bar Room*, is a propagandist classic, and is still in print.

It is gratifying to notice that the eminent Victorian novelists are emerging somewhat from the smoke-screen of disparagement that has kept them pretty well out of view, especially in our academic circles, for the last twenty-five years. They cannot be said to have come into their own, precisely, for they are not read by us to any extent; our literary preoccupations with the present and the future are too exacting—and too muddling—to allow that. But there seems to be a fairly general consciousness that with due allowance made for certain broad streaks of obvious, one may almost say conventional, foible, the principal novelists of the Nineteenth Century, in its middle and later decades, were deuced whal-

ing big people, as British slang might put it. Their literary
faults and failings were as conspicuous and distinct as their
excellences, and as persistent; they did not move along for
great stretches of composition on a dead level of fair-to-
middling. Hugo, for example, was about half the time genius,
half the time charlatan, but he was equally great at both; he
was all there in either character, and entirely, blissfully un-
selfconscious about his appearance in either character; one
would say that he never really knew, at any given moment,
which of the two he was assuming. This it is that gives to
his *History of a Crime*, for instance, a quality possessed, I sincerely believe, by no other book on earth. One laughs most
indecorously all the way through it; it is one of the funniest
compositions ever penned by man; and yet, all the time one
is laughing, one is possessed completely by immense indignation and outrage at what is described there and by immense
respect for the genius that describes it.

Here, then, we have the ideal subject matter for parody,
and Harte deals with it in a manner worthy of his subject.
Les Misérables, the reader will remember, has a dozen lines
of preface in which Hugo is charlatan complete and perfect,
of purest ray serene. Let the reader peruse it carefully, and
then turn to this, with which Harte prefaces his parody:

As long as there shall exist three paradoxes, a moral
Frenchman, a religious atheist and a believing sceptic; so
long, in fact, as booksellers shall wait—say twenty-five
years—for a new gospel; so long as paper shall remain
cheap and ink three *sous* a bottle; I have no hesitation in
saying that such books as these are not utterly profitless.

Nothing could be better. Dickens's foibles and mannerisms,
his mannerisms of mind as well as of style, are writ large and
unselfconsciously on his pages; his weakness, as in the case

of the other great Victorians, was set off most conspicuously against his strength, so that there could be no doubt or critical tergiversation about it. Harte, then, has this:

He sat alone in a gloomy library, listening to the wind that roared in the chimney. Around him novels and storybooks were strewn thickly; in his lap he held one with its pages freshly cut, and turned the leaves wearily until his eyes rested upon a portrait in its frontispiece. And as the wind howled the more fiercely, and the darkness without fell blacker, a strange and fateful likeness to that portrait appeared above his chair and leaned upon his shoulder. The Haunted Man gazed at the portrait and sighed. The figure gazed at the portrait and sighed too.

"Here again?" said the Haunted Man.

"Here again," it repeated in a low voice.

"Another novel?"

"Another novel."

"The old story?"

"The old story."

"I see a child," said the Haunted Man, gazing from the pages of the book into the fire, "a most unnatural child, a model infant. It is prematurely old and philosophic. It dies in poverty to slow music. It dies surrounded by luxury to slow music. It dies with an accompaniment of golden water and rattling carts to slow music. Previous to its decease it makes a will; it repeats the Lord's Prayer, it kisses the 'boofer lady.' That child——"

"Is mine," said the phantom.

"I see a good woman, undersized. I see several charming women, but they are all undersized. They are more or less imbecile and idiotic, but always fascinating and undersized. They wear coquettish caps and aprons. I observe that feminine virtue is invariably below the medium height, and that it is always simple and infantine. These women——"

"Are mine."

"I see a haughty, proud and wicked lady. She is tall and queenly. I remark that all proud and wicked women are tall and queenly. That woman——"

"Is mine," said the phantom, wringing its hands.

"I see several things continually impending. I observe that whenever an accident, a murder or death is about to happen, there is something in the furniture, in the locality, in the atmosphere, that foreshadows and suggests it years in advance. I cannot say that in real life I have noticed it; the perception of this surprising fact belongs——"

"To me," said the phantom. The Haunted Man continued in a despairing tone:

"I see the influence of this in the magazines and daily papers. I see weak imitators rise up and enfeeble the world with senseless formula. I am getting tired of it. It won't do, Charles! it won't do," and the Haunted Man buried his head in his hands and groaned.

Comparing Harte's book with Sir Owen Seaman's little volume called *Borrowed Plumes*, we see clearly how Harte's instinct for the choice of great subjects stood by him. Sir Owen Seaman is a highly gifted parodist, but he simply had nothing to parody; the contemporary writers whom he parodied were too slight and insubstantial for anyone to parody with anything like a classic resulting. Harte's superiority comes out again in his keeping his work free from caricature. With all his keen discernment of weaknesses and absurdity, he never fails to communicate the sense that he is dealing with a great subject. In fact if I were trying to interest a modern student in these distinguished Victorians, I am not sure but that I would approach the task by way of Harte's parodies. One who reads *Miss Mix*, Harte's parody on *Jane Eyre*, will find Miss Brontë's preposterous ineptitudes and absurdities faithfully reflected, but yet he will get the impression that somehow, nevertheless, *Jane Eyre* manages to be a highly considerable piece of work. In *The Dweller of the Threshold* one confronts all the pinchbeck writing, all the baroque transcendentalism; in *Lothair* one confronts the tireless climber and insatiable toadeater; but one cannot quite get away from the conviction that as literary men, Disraeli and Lord Lytton were extremely respectable figures, notwithstanding. Here is Alexandre Dumas in the raw, at the conclusion of *The Ninety-nine Guardsmen:*

Suddenly the ladder was lifted two feet from below. This enabled the king to leap in the window. At the farther end of the apartment stood a young girl, with red hair and a lame leg. She was trembling with emotion.

"Louise!"

"The King!"

"Ah, my God, mademoiselle."

"Ah, my God, sire."

But a low knock at the door interrupted the lovers. The King uttered a cry of rage; Louise one of despair.

The door opened and d'Artagnan entered.

"Good-evening, sire," said the musketeer.

The King touched a bell. Porthos appeared in the doorway.

"Good-evening, sire."

"Arrest M. d'Artagnan."

Porthos looked at d'Artagnan and did not move.

The King almost turned purple with rage. He again touched the bell. Athos entered.

"Count, arrest Porthos and d'Artagnan."

The Count de la Fère glanced at Porthos and d'Artagnan, and smiled sweetly.

"Sacré! Where is Aramis?" said the King, violently.

"Here, sire," and Aramis entered.

"Arrest Athos, Porthos and d'Artagnan."

"Arrest yourself."

The King shuddered and turned pale. "Am I not King of France?"

"Assuredly, sire, but we are also severally Porthos, Aramis, d'Artagnan and Athos."

"Ah!" said the King.

"Yes, sire."

"What does this mean?"

"It means, your Majesty," said Aramis, stepping forward, "that your conduct as a married man is highly improper. I am an Abbé, and I object to these improprieties. My good friends here, d'Artagnan, Athos and Porthos, pure-minded young men, are terribly shocked. Observe, sire, how they blush!"

Athos, Porthos and d'Artagnan blushed.

"Ah," said the King, thoughtfully, "you teach me a lesson. You are devoted and noble young gentlemen, but your only weakness is your excessive modesty. From this moment I make you all marshals and dukes, with the exception of Aramis."

"And me, sire?" said Aramis.

"You shall be an archbishop."

The four friends looked up and then rushed into each other's arms. The King embraced Louise de la Vallière by way of keeping them company. A pause ensued. At last Athos spoke:

"Swear, my children, that next to yourselves, you will respect the King of France; and remember that 'forty years after' we will meet again."

Yes, this is indeed a very lifelike Dumas, and by no means a caricature. If I might reproduce the entire parody, I believe that with all its keen penetration it would still carry the conviction that Dumas was a valid and substantial literary quantity; that if one wished to cultivate Dumas, one might get a prepossessing and appetizing foretaste of him from the flavor of Harte's work.

As Harte avoided caricature, so also he avoided burlesque. He did not tell his own story or introduce his own literary notions or his own style. To make the distinction clear, one may place any specimen of his work beside the best and most delightful burlesque that ever has come my way, which is Thackeray's *Rowena and Rebecca*. There Thackeray had an idea of his own to work out, and an excellent one it was. He was dissatisfied with the novelist's habit of abandoning the hero and heroine at the marriage altar; there was a good deal of life to be lived after marriage, and some of it doubtless interesting. He was especially dissatisfied when Sir Walter Scott ended his novel with the marriage of Ivanhoe and Rowena, for he thought that Rowena was a very poor affair, not being good enough for Ivanhoe. "Must the Disinherited Knight, whose blood has been fired by the suns of Palestine, and whose heart has been warmed in the company of the tender and beautiful Rebecca, sit down contented for life by the side of such a frigid piece of propriety as that icy, faultless, prim, niminy-piminy Rowena? Forbid it fate, forbid it poetical justice!"

When one thinks of it, indeed, the question is natural and searching. So Thackeray set out on a sequel to Ivanhoe, to get the matter reasonably adjusted. But he does not imitate Scott; he tells his own story in his own style—and the story is captivating, the style is rare and rich. He has no concern with Sir Walter's mannerisms or with bringing Sir Walter at all before the reader's consciousness. Even by indirection. He deals, that is, in pure burlesque. Harte, on the other hand, is concerned exclusively with the author and does not engage the reader's mind upon any idea, story or style of his own; he deals in pure parody.

The foregoing, as I said, does not pretend to be a critical treatment of Harte in his capacity of parodist, but only a

brief and partial intimation of a few points that would naturally come up in such a treatment of him, if one were ever
made. One could easily establish him, I think, as the best of
all parodists—one could do it, probably, by no more than an
elaboration of the points of superiority that I have noted, and
no doubt it is worth doing. I cite his case merely in support
of a different contention. His *Condensed Novels* is something
that we are likely to miss—we whose connection with literature is unprofessional—which most of us have missed, and in
missing it have missed a good deal that is both interesting and
formative. I believe our loss is largely due to our being too
exclusively forward-looking in our survey of our literature;
and this is due in great part to the fashion set by the nationalist spirit. My suggestion is, therefore, that criticism disregard flatly both the fashion and the spirit that sets it. Criticism's business is with a good thing, wherever found, and
whether it has to look in one direction for it, or in another,
is quite immaterial. Criticism's business distinctly is not to go
out to service to nationalism or to heed the fashions that nationalism dictates for its own purposes; and if criticism is
unconsciously falling in with these, it should feel with gratitude the wakening hand of anyone who has noticed its aber-
ration.

THE PURPOSE OF BIOGRAPHY

WHAT IS biography for? What useful purpose does it serve? Why should one write it? What is its actual importance in the field of literature? Above all, what is autobiography for, and what proper motive might one have for writing it?'

I put these questions to one of my literary acquaintances the other day, in the hope of clearing my own mind. It has once or twice been suggested to me (as I suppose it has been suggested to everybody who has ever published anything) that I should write the biography of this-or-that eminent person. My instinct promptly jibbed at the suggestion; and in each case, after dallying with the idea awhile, I threw it over. Then latterly, while looking into one or two current biographies, I was moved to wonder what prompted my instinct. Was it the consciousness of incapacity or of laziness or of both? Probably both, to a degree; yet I thought there must be a little more to it than that, because I had already caught myself pondering the question why these biographies had been written. I could not see that they served any purpose worth serving; they seemed to me to be addressed mostly to a vulgar and prying inquisitiveness; and this in turn led me to raise the questions which I subsequently put to my literary friend.

We finally agreed, my friend and I, that the legitimate function of modern biography (and *a fortiori* of autobiography) is to help the historian. We recalled the fact that biography, as now understood, is comparatively a new thing in our literature. Neither of us could put our finger on an example of it earlier than the seventeenth century. In principle, modern biography is an objective account of the life of one man. It begins with his birth, ends with his death, and includes every item of detail which has any actual or probable historical significance. All collateral matter which goes in by way of 'setting' should be cut down to what is in distinct and direct relation to that one man. In principle, above all, modern biography admits of nothing tendentious, nor does it admit of the puffing out or slighting of detail to any degree beyond what the author, in all good faith and conscience, believes the historical importance of that detail would warrant.

If biographical practice followed principle, obviously, fewer biographies would be written, far fewer autobiographies, and far fewer of either would be generally read; the only person likely to profit by them would be the historian. Things being as they are, however, commerical considerations intervene between principle and practice, as they always do. Publishers look with a jaundiced eye on a biography which in their view is not "readable"; and their view of what is readable is set by what experience has shown to be the terms of popular demand. The author, under a double pressure to produce a readable book—for most authors are not above some little thought of profit—sees that the satisfaction of these terms is quite incompatible with a devotion to principle, and proceeds accordingly.

Hence, as a rule, the actual practice of modern biography is heavily sophisticated in response to the extremely unwholesome terms of a lively popular demand for that type of literature. Like our practice of fiction, it aims to hit the lowest common denominator of taste and intelligence among its potential public. This procedure is bad. For the writer, it is bad in two ways. First, because it tempts him to pick subjects which, from the historical point of view, are not worth a biography; and this category, as I shall presently show, includes some of the most eminent names. Second, the current low conception of what makes a book readable tempts him continually to a culpable misplacement of emphasis among the various orders of fact with which he deals. To cite an extreme instance, some time ago I read a wretched misshapen sketch of a great musician's life. All I got out of it which I did not already know was that this musician had the habit of using very filthy language. Evidences of this habit were scattered so overliberally throughout the volume as to make one think the thing had been written expressly to air them.

For the reader as well as the writer, the sophistication of biography is bad; and this also in two ways. First, because it acquaints the public, often with great overemphasis, with a variety of matters which not only are devoid of historical significance, but also are preëminently none of the public's business. This stiffens the reader in his congenital resentment of privacy, his share in the vulgar assumption, so odiously overdeveloped in the United States and so powerfully encouraged by the dominant influences in our public life—the assumption that anybody's doings are everybody's business by full right and title. I do not speak of matters which might be thought questionable, but of those in general which are in their nature one's own concern, and none other's. If the subject "wore a checked shirt and a number-nine shoe, and had a pink wart on his nose," he was within his rights; it was nobody's business, the fact has no historical value whatever, and a disquisition on it, however "readable," has no place in a biography.

Second, the vogue of commercial biography is bad for the reader because it fosters the erroneous notion that knowing something *about* a subject, or even knowing a great deal about him, is the same thing, or just as good, as knowing the subject himself; and here comes in the case of those biographers whose subject is simply not worth a biography, and will not support one. To know Thoreau, for example, is an inestimable privilege, and anyone may have it; it is got in the most direct and simplest possible way by reading his works, and it cannot be got in any other way. All that is worth anyone's knowing *about* Thoreau can be got in five minutes out of any good encyclopædia. Reading the biographical portions of Mr. Canby's recent book, therefore, if I may say so, makes one feel like Mr. Weller's charity-boy at the end of the alphabet. Among other matters, for instance, Mr. Canby has dredged up evidence tending to show that Thoreau was not indifferent to female society; well, what of it? The fact, if it be a fact, has no historical importance; and either in liking the ladies or in disliking them he was quite within his rights, and it is none of the public's business. It may be said that the curiosity stirred by this order of research will egg people on to reading Thoreau, and thus put them in the way of actually knowing him. This seems to me highly improbable; they are far more likely to rest on an *Ersatz*-knowledge vamped up out of what Mr. Canby tells them, and let it go at that. In fact, I suspect that the popular appetite for "readable" biography is symptomatic not only of a low and prurient curiosity, but also, when this motive is not dominant, of a wish to live exclusively on predigested cultural food, which no one can do. A passive and workless *Ersatz*-knowledge of illustrious men seems to me to reflect our national ideals of a passive and workless *Ersatz*-education, a passive and workless *Ersatz*-culture; ideals which we are beginning to see are illusory.

In the case of any subject, no matter how eminent, most of the minutiæ of his day-to-day existence are of no earthly importance to the historian. Even at this early date Lord Morley's biography of Gladstone, a classical example, free from any taint of commercialism, reminds us that Time is a great winnower, and we are driven to wonder whether some other literary form might in general be more serviceable; or whether, as a compromise measure, an alternative might be found in amending our practice by laying down the rule that a subject's private activities, his character, and his relations of whatever kind, are insignificant except as they affect his public activities, character and relations, and that the sound biographer should distribute his space accordingly.

Matters which are in themselves minutiæ may take on an adventitious importance to the historian by reason of consequences accruing from them to the public. There can be no doubt of that. Disregard of it is what has vitiated a great deal of earlier biography, and has led to the vogue of debunking, now happily on the wane. Unless the subject is contemporary, however, or nearly so, the biographer is in as good a position as the historian to understand this and to make all proper discriminations. A sound biographer of Priam's son, for example, would anticipate the historian of Ilium with a pretty full account of his dallyings with the skittish Helen; so, *mutatis mutandis,* would a sound biographer of Louis XV, or of Napoleon III. On the other hand, none of the first Napoleon's adventures in Mrs. Chikno's "roving and uncertificated line," though they seem to have been both enterprising and extensive, is worth a button to history, and therefore the sound biographer would finish off the whole assortment in about three agate lines. That George Washington was a man of sin—that he swore, drank whiskey, gambled, went to dances, infested the theatre, chased the light-o'-loves, smoked cigarettes, or whatever it was that the debunkers lay to his charge—this seems to have had no bearing on his public activities, and is therefore nothing for the sound biographer to waste space on. That he was a land-speculator and land-jobber did bear heavily on his public activities, and a sound biographer would take all due notice of it.

Matthew Arnold left an explicit request that he should not be the subject of a biography. No doubt his unfailing critical sense told him that there was nothing in the circumstances of his life to make a biography worth the paper it was written on. A recent effort made in disregard of his wish—and made, one must say, in execrably bad taste—shows clearly that this may well have been the case. Like Thoreau, he was a public figure in but one capacity, that of a man of letters. One may know him intimately and profitably through his works— there is no other way—but what one may know or not know *about* him is of no importance. Joseph Butler, the great bishop of Durham, took extraordinary care to baffle what we who are bred on the ideals of journalism and the cinema call "personal publicity." All that is known *about* him is that he rode around his diocese on a black pony, rode very fast, and was scandalously imposed upon by beggars. Yet one may know Butler intimately, say through the *Rolls Sermons,* and thereby make a valuable acquaintance, even for these days of so much supposititious enlightenment on religious matters. I have often thought it is unfortunate that so many of us are contemptuous of "the old religion" without knowing the best that the old religion could do. Knowing the Goethe of the *Conversations* is an imperishable benefit, but how much is there to know about Goethe that is worth knowing or is anyone's business to know? I think very little. Recent publications have settled me in the firm belief that one who knows Ruskin, Emerson, Coleridge, intimately, but knows nothing about them, is far ahead of one who knows all about them, but does not know them. Knowing Homer and Shakespeare is certainly something; but all that anyone actually knows about Shakespeare can be written on a postcard, and nobody knows even where or when Homer was born.

All I have been saying about biography bears with even greater force on autobiography because it is harder to assess the actual importance of one's own doings and adventures in life than it is to deal in the same disinterested fashion with those of others. There is greater difficulty in drawing the line firmly between matters of legitimate private interest and those of legitimate public interest. My friend Mr. Villard's recent book called *Fighting Years* is of great value to the historian of his period—I know of none more valuable—but only after Mr. Villard does finally get around to talking about his fighting years. What precedes this (counting in a few later lapses from objectivity) comes roughly to a fourth of the book; it deals with matters which are of highly justifiable interest to Mr. Villard and his family, to me and the rest of his friends, but which are of no legitimate interest to the public —they are indeed none of the public's business. One wishes that Mr. Villard had resolutely forgone all notion of an autobiography, struck into his subject at the point where his fighting years began, and cast his book in the form of memoirs. As an inveterate reformer, if he had wished—as I think he might well have done—to show "how he got that way," he could have done it easily in an introductory paragraph.

I have seen in my time—a rather long time, as man's life goes—only one specimen of this type of literature which seemed to me flawless. One could do no better than let it serve as a structural model for both biography and autobiography, and I therefore feel justified in speaking of it somewhat at length as such. I came on it only lately, about six months ago. It is not the work of a writer, a man of letters, or even one of more than moderate literary attainments. It is the work of a Russian musician.

II

Rimsky-Korsakov, Nikolai Andreyevitch, commenced his autobiography in 1876, when he was thirty-two years old. He ended it in 1906, two years before his death. He worked at it at long intervals; ten years elapsed between the first and second chapters, six between the second and third, eleven between the seventh and eighth. He died in 1908; his widow brought out the book in 1909, suppressing certain passages, and a second edition came out in 1910. An English translation, said to be excellent, was made by Mr. Joffe from this second edition, and was published, I think in 1923, by Mr. A. A. Knopf. I have not seen it. A third Russian edition appeared in 1928, edited by the composer's son, Andrei Nikolaivitch, who restored the passages which had been cut out of the two editions preceding.

Like Thoreau, Rimsky-Korsakov was in one capacity, and one only, a public figure. In all other respects his life, like Thoreau's, had not a single feature of legitimate interest to the public. The first signal merit of his book lies in its clear, consistent consciousness that the public was entitled to the fullest information about everything which bore directly or indirectly on the author's character and activities as a musician, and was not entitled to any information about anything which had any other bearing. The book's fidelity to this sound principle is amazing. My copy of it runs to three hundred closely-printed pages, and I have scanned it line by line for some sign of departure or wavering, but I have not found one.

The domestic "setting" of the author's birth and infancy is a matter of ten lines. His father played the piano (an old one) by ear; so did an uncle, who could not read music, but was "very musical," though the father seems to have had the better musical memory. The author's mother habitually slowed down the tempo of the songs she sang to him in his childhood; this was an "odd trait," and the author has the notion that he may have inherited this tendency from her. This is all we are told of either parent's biography. He does not mention the name of his father or mother, or say a word about their families or forebears. In the second chapter he gives his father a paragraph of praise, but it is only by way of showing that, in spite of their *ancien régime* distaste for a musical career, his parents disinterestedly did their best for him.

The author had a wife, "an excellent musician," and has nothing to say about her in any other capacity. He does mention her name, but he had to do that in order to distinguish her from a sister who was a singer; she was a pianiste, and they often appeared together. He had children; the birth of a son gets half a line. They are brought into the narrative only as some incident—for example, the illness of a son or the death of a daughter—had this-or-that effect on some musical project which was under way. The incident itself gets bare mention; we do not know what ailed the boy or what carried off the girl. The author's own indispositions are brought in vaguely to account for some difficulty with his music; "pain in the head, a feeling of pressure," worried him at the Marinsky's rehearsal of his fairy-ballet *Mlada*. There is collateral evidence that the author was genuinely fond of the four friends and comrades who had valiantly weathered through the terrible *Sturm und Drang* period of Russian music in the last quarter of the century; yet see how the book takes the death of the one perhaps closest to him:

> On the sixteenth of February, 1887, very early in the morning, I was taken by surprise when V. V. Stassov came to my door in a great state of agitation, saying "Borodin is dead!" . . . I shall not describe the emotion of us all. What would become of *Prince Igor* and his other incomplete or unpublished works? Stassov and I went at once to the dead man's apartment, and carried off all his manuscripts to my house.

Twice, in going through the book, the reader may think he has caught the author napping, but he will be wrong. In the first chapter Rimsky-Korsakov has a bit to say about his love for the sea, and about an older brother who is a lieutenant in the navy. This seems irrelevant, but in the next chapter we find the author himself in the Naval College, on his way to becoming an officer; and this in turn is introductory to the account of sixteen years of effort to drive the two careers in double harness, and of the one's reactions upon the other. Again, in the sixteenth chapter he waxes lyrical to the extent of nine lines, praising rural joys of the truly old-fashioned Russian village of Stelovo, where he spent the summer of 1880; but you see the point when you turn a page and discover that in those two-and-a-half months he composed the whole of *Snegourotchka*. Writing in the period 1894-1896, almost at the end of his life, he says that "up to this present time I have never finished off any work so easily and rapidly." He recalled the delights of Stelovo because they had a conspicuous bearing on music. The trees, the river, fruits, flowers, the incessant song of birds—"all this was in some sort of harmony with my leanings towards pantheism, and my love for the subject of *Snegourotchka*."

Another merit of the book, as great as the first, is born of the author's clear understanding that its sole function is that of helping the historian of Russian music. Everything that would help the historian is there, and nothing is there which would confuse him, waste his eyesight, or arouse his distrust. To show that this is so would take more space than I can afford. I can only suggest that those who are thinking of doing something with biography should get a copy of the book and make a careful study of it from this point of view.

But to help the historian, the biographer must be objective; he must resolutely keep prepossession from laying traps for the historian's feet. The third great merit of Rimsky-Korsakov's book is that it perfectly meets this requirement; one does not see how objectivity could be carried further. This is the more remarkable, perhaps, because the book, like Mr. Villard's, is a record of "fighting years." It deals with a violent æsthetic rebellion which Mr. Ernest Newman, in his superb *Musical Critic's Holiday*, admirably compares with the great Florentine revolt against musical orthodoxy in

1600; yet nowhere in the book can I find the trace of a single biased judgment, a single prepossession. I would have the intending biographer go through it once more, and study it carefully from this point of view.

A fourth signal merit is that Rimsky-Korsakov always "comes across." He never butters up a person or a situation, and on the other hand, he never exaggerates anything unfavorable to either. He says exactly all that should be said, but never a word more. In this respect his work stands in vivid and gratifying contrast to all the attempts at autobiography that I have seen in recent years; they do not quite come across. The five Russian rebels were very young, going on for thirty; being young, they were ardent, irrepressible, aggressive. The leading spirit, Balakirev, was the only one who could pretend to anything like a professional knowledge of music, and he had next to none. Let the reader notice Rimsky-Korsakov's treatment of Balakirev throughout, and especially the marvelous summing-up of his influence on his comrades. The others were rank amateurs; two of them were notable, however, in their proper professions. The half-French Cui was a distinguished engineer-officer in the army, and Borodin was a distinguished physician and chemist. Moussorgsky was an officer in the Preobrazhensky regiment, but presently left the army, and became a functionary in the civil service, in the Department of Forests.[1] Not one of them was a trained musician. They really did not know what they wanted, what they were driving at, and knew even less of how to drive at it. To deal disinterestedly with matters like these is something of an achievement—let the reader observe how Rimsky-Korsakov deals with them. Not a word is said about anyone's personal character, qualities or habits,

---

[1] Mr. Virgil Thomson, in his recent book, *The State of Music*, says that Cui was a chemist and Moussorgsky a customs official. This is a curious error, but trivial, hardly worth noticing, because the only point is that neither man was a professional musician, and Mr. Thomson makes this point clearly.—AUTHOR

except as bearing on music; then what is said is said in full, and with complete objectivity. Balakirev went to pieces, Moussorgsky drank too much, Borodin's household was in continual disorder; well, that was that, and its effect upon their productivity was such-and-such. Alone among critics, Stassov gave the rebels enthusiastic support; its effect was this-and-that. He had certain critical defects; the outcome of them was so-and-so.

III

Is it perhaps possible that our writers are overdoing biography a little? Is not autobiography, coarsened and discolored by commercialism as it is, being rather recklessly overdone among us? I fear so. I have before me now a letter from someone who proposes to write a biography of a personage whom I used to know slightly. The prospect depresses me, for to my certain knowledge that personage, like Thoreau, will simply not support a biography. The utmost that can be expected is that this intending biographer will produce, *Gott soll hüten*, one more "readable" book, one more windfall for the book clubs or a likely bid for the Pulitzer prize; and this, as Rabelais says of an enterprise essentially similar, is a terrible thing to think upon.

All the more so because meanwhile other literary forms, quite as respectable and far more appropriate, go begging. If some aspect of a subject's public career strikes you as possibly fruitful, why not write an essay about it, as Mr. Brooks did in his *Ordeal of Mark Twain?* The essay-form is greatly neglected; yet a critical essay on Thoreau, for example, one such as Matthew Arnold wrote on Gray and on Wordsworth, would be worth a dozen inevitably abortive attempts at a biography. There are innumerable great essays to be written about great American figures as seen in the light of the present time. At this point in the course of our public affairs, for example, what would more powerfully conduce to a competent understanding of our political selves and our political condition than such an essay on John Adams as Walter Bagehot would write; or what more to a salutary sense of our spiritual decrepitude than an essay on Emerson such as Ernest Renan, Scherer or Sainte-Beuve would write—or, indeed, an essay on that same Thoreau?

If, again, you are interested in a subject's standards of personal character and conduct, write a study of them. If you have been a close observer of great affairs, or of affairs which if not great are amusing, unusual, interesting, picaresque, write memoirs. The best and most useful book of memoirs that I ever saw was anonymous; the author almost never spoke of himself. It came out in 1892, entitled *An Englishman in Paris*. I wish Mr. Villard had done something like that; it would have had the ingratiating and persuasive literary quality which, owing to the autobiographical form, his work now falls just short of having. If your observations and reflections seem worth printing, print your diary; it is the best literary form for the purpose—Blunt's diary and the Goncourts' are gold mines for the historian. All these literary forms seem to me as sorely neglected by us as the biographical form seems sorely overworked.

But people will not read essays, memoirs, studies, diaries, and therefore publishers will not touch them, especially if offered by obscure or unpopular authors; people want biography. It may be a little indelicate to say so, but on this point it seems to me that the testimony of an author who is both obscure and unpopular might be worth something. All I have ever written has been in one or another of these forms, and I have somehow managed to get it published; and there is evidence that many more people read it than I would have dared think were likely to do so. Hence I am far from sure that this prejudice of public and publishers is as strong as it is supposed to be. I have sometimes wondered whether the book market would actually collapse if authors and publishers declared a general strike on the biographical form. I doubt it. I know a pampered cat named Thomas, who turns his back on any kind of food but liver, and will have none of it—for a while—but when he finds his choice dealt down to fish or nothing, he takes fish and likes it. On a similar choice, the pampered public might take something besides biography and get it down without too much retching. However that may be, publishers and authors might at least unite on the less radical measure of tightening up the practice of biography a little. If an author must write biography, let him write it on something like correct principles. If it is positively decreed in the council of the gods that he shall write an autobiography, let him write one like Rimsky-Korsakov's.

THE KING'S JESTER:
MODERN STYLE

In the old days, before the king business went into practical liquidation, the court jester was an established institution. This functionary's job required him not only to be entertaining, but also realistic; in fact, his success at entertainment was pretty strictly conditioned by his sense of reality. All the other court functionaries cooked up the king's facts for him before delivery; the jester delivered them raw. This was the curious convention of the time. The jester was the only person permitted to tell the king the plain, unupholstered truth about things as he saw them, even about royalty itself and the most intimate matters pertaining to royalty; and he was not only permitted but expected to do this. The jester criticized State policies in a full-mouthed way that would have insured anybody else a life sojourn in the bastille; and he got praise and favor for it. He could tell the king that his favorite mistress was a mercenary old rip who should be thrown to the sharks and, as our phrase goes, he could get away with it, and be applauded for it, which no one else could do, either in the court or in the kingdom at large.

Historically, I believe, nobody knows how this peculiar institution grew up, or where it came from. It may have arisen out of the fundamental need of human nature for an occasional contact with fact and truth. A king was a vertebrated animal, like anyone else; and as such he could not live by pretense alone. Once in a while, probably, he had to brace up on a little refreshing go at fact and truth. But he could not approach fact and truth *seriously* because of their highly explosive quality. They might go off at any moment, and blow the political edifice into the air. His official or serious contacts could be only with pretense, because pretense was the foundation of the whole regime of absolutism. The institution of the jester, therefore, enabled royalty to have its fling, upon the strict conventional understanding that it should not "count," that the experience should be merely exhilarating, and not translatable into purpose and action.

In another respect, too, the jester was exempt from the regular rules of court etiquette. It seems from old accounts that he could mix around promiscuously with everybody, high, low, rich, and poor. He was at home everywhere, in palace or hovel, and everybody made much of him in ways that must have helped him out a good deal in the discharge of his function. Nobody ever put up a front with the jester; he always saw people as pretty much their natural selves. Thus he gravitated into the confidence of the general run of folks and learned what they were thinking about. This was likely to make him—and often did make him—a good interpreter of the popular mind. He spoke with the people's voice and in the tone of popular opinion and judgment.

In a republic the people are sovereign, nominally and perhaps really. But as far as the republican principle has as yet been worked out, it has mostly taken over and recostumed the main essentials of the old order and put them at work again quite in the old way. The French and American Revolutions made absolutism step aside only long enough to change its clothes in decent privacy, before resuming its place at the old stand. Make-believe remains as the foundation and chief working asset of the new political system, as it was of the old. Under these circumstances it is highly interesting to observe that the many-headed sovereign seems to show the same old need for occasional contact with fact and truth that the single-headed sovereign used to show, and that the republican system has set up a device whereby he can make it on the same old terms. This device, exactly like that of the king's jester, embodies a strict convention. It enables the many-headed monarch to make his contact with fact and truth on the clear and careful undertaking that it shall not count, that he shall not take the experience seriously as something translatable into purpose and action.

This republican counterpart of the king's jester is the newspaper-paragrapher and paragrapher-cartoonist. His development, and the privileged character of his position in our system, constitute one of the most impressive curiosities of modern journalism. No more exact parallel to the primitive institution could be devised. The paragrapher has inherited all the jester's privileges, neither more nor fewer, and exactly the same set of expectations are put upon him. The freer his speech to the sovereign lord, the closer and shrewder his approach to the plain natural truth of things, the more he is appreciated and applauded. The wider his experience of human nature and the closer his interpretations come to the residual common sense of mankind, the more firmly, by common consent, he is fixed in his job. The more profound and subversive his implications, the stronger his position at the republican sovereign's court. Moreover, there is no one to contest or to share his privileges; he is a unique figure in a unique function. If the prophet, the publicist, the professor, lecturer, or so-called public servant undertook to assume his liberties and prerogatives he would at once come to grief in an avalanche of general disapproval.

II

It has amused me for some time to keep more or less consecutive track of our paragraphers and to weigh their utterances critically. I began this practice during the War. Being in Europe a good deal at the time, and in a position which made it desirable for me to have accurate knowledge of what was really going on, I began to pay great and increasing heed to the paragraphers; with such good results that I suppose I can say I am the only observer of that period who put practically his whole dependence on the comic papers. In all countries, long before I waded through statesmen's speeches and publicists' deliverances, I assembled all the comic papers I could get my hands on, and studied them prayerfully. I may say, too (for it is in praise of my authorities and not of myself) that I know of no observer who came out right oftener than I did, whether in an estimate of the present or a forecast of the future. Since then I have kept up the practice and got big dividends out of it. When I wish an interpretation or an illumination of the day's news I turn to the paragraphers for it, not to the editorial writers. After all, this is quite in the tradition. If the oldtime king had let the jester take the measure of things for him and acted on it he would have mostly come out better than he did, because the jester was the most experienced and disinterested person he had about him, and —most important of all—entirely unanswerable to the general conventions of the court.

It is not generally realized, I believe, that the paragrapher has so significant a position among us at the present time; indeed, without a rather attentive analysis of his work, it could probably not be realized. Yet the realization is useful, if only to reveal to ourselves the lengths we unconsciously go in our subscription to pretense and make-believe; and the best way to get it is by free discussion of some examples.

Among the extracts from the press that I have lately potted I find the following:

> You can't expect a professional politician to make up his bed and then lie on it. He's more likely to make up his bunk and then lie out of it.

This is a perfect example of the jester's license, exercised at the expense of his fellow-courtiers; it is the product of a shrewd, experienced, realistic mind. Its implications are profound and subversive and, put in this way, or rather, under these privileged conditions, they are wholly acceptable to the many-headed sovereign. In them he feels the welcome contact with fact and truth. But he cannot take his experience seriously because the whole array of protective convention thrown over our political system forbids it. If there were any question of his taking it seriously, indeed, he would rise up in royal indignation and declare that he had never had any such experience, but on the contrary was much annoyed by the jester's presumption, and would go promptly after his scalp.

A little imagination will show the truth of this. The implications of this paragraph are that politicians, of whatever stripe, school, or party, are lying, swindling fellows, untrustworthy and inconsiderable, and out for their own purposes. Exactly the same implications appear in another paragraph, which I put beside it:

The crookedest politics is always measured by the plum line.

Utterances like these, subversive as they are, never attract the royal disapproval; they never lose the paper that prints them a single subscriber. In fact, if they are frequent enough and pungent enough, they are a good circulation-getter. But now imagine any newspaper taking their implications seriously and molding its news-policy and editorial policy upon them! Suppose, say, that the Baltimore *Sun* should decide to go before the sovereign public in a perfectly realistic attitude towards politics and politicians of all parties—which is exactly the attitude appearing in these two paragraphs! I do not mean that the paper should inveigh against politics in every issue, or be always calling politicians liars and swindlers, but simply that it consistently give its entire treatment of politics, both in news and editorial form, the precise "slant" of those two paragraphs. What would be the consequence? Practically every one of those who now accept the jester's implications, who know that the jester has quite perfectly hit off their own convictions and made himself the echo of their own consciousness, even reflecting back to them their own tone and temper, would get into a great state of indignation and resentment over the republican equivalent of lese-majesty, and would stop their subscription.

An effective paragrapher in one of our most prominent newspapers makes this observation on the course of American imperialism:

An American syndicate is bidding for a concession to extract the salts from the Dead Sea. Which suggests the difficulty of landing marines near this inland sea for the purpose of protecting American lives and property.

Another paper of almost equal prominence has the following on the same general topic:

RICH GOLD STRIKE MADE IN PHILIPPINES
Nature seems determined not to have those islands independent.

Now, what newspaper can safely reproduce upon its news policy and editorial policy the implications of these remarks? One thinks at once of the late Frank A. Munsey moving about among his editorial writers, saying, "Now, no opinions! Remember—no opinions!" Yet everyone is aware—everyone who has enough intelligence to be aware of anything—that these paragraphs imply the plain natural truth about the dinosaurian progress of the imperialism begun under Mr. Jefferson in the Louisiana tract, and continued in the

Floridas and the various Indian territories, in Texas, the Northwest, the Coast, Hawaii, the Philippines, and latterly in the Caribbean. The many-headed sovereign thus has his refreshing and relieving approach to fact and truth, but he cannot for a moment take it seriously; the consequences would be ruinous. His serious approach to the topic of imperialism in the case of the Philippines, for example, must be made with reverential regard to convention, by way of such guarded writing as I saw lately in an editorial on the subject, or such as anyone can see in any editorial—it is stereotyped—about the necessity of holding the Filipinos in leash indefinitely for their own good, and in order to instruct them "how to develop their natural resources in an orderly and profitable manner."

When an election comes on we all know how convention presides over any avenue of serious approach to the subject. The volume and character of news-writing, editorial-writing, feature-writing, personality sketches, the broadcasting of speeches, and so on, conspire to represent this event as something of enormous moment. The "issues of the campaign" are conventionally scrutinized, and a strictly conventional attitude maintained towards the pledges and promises of the several candidates or parties. The other day I noticed the work of a paragrapher-cartoonist, entitled, "Another Gas War Looming." It showed a voter in a Ford car, pulled up in the midst of half a dozen filling-stations labelled, "High Test Promises," "Economy Promises," "More Miles per Taxes," and such like, with a vociferous candidate standing beside each one, imploring patronage. The voter's soliloquy was, "Well, I oughtn't to have any trouble getting 'filled up' with all these filling-stations around." Here the American sovereign gets the realistic rather than the conventional line of approach to the national event. It falls in precisely with his intuitive sense of the plain natural truth of things, but he dare not admit that it does, even to himself. His appreciation of the experience is strictly within the limits set by convention; and herein once more he is precisely on a level footing with the kings of old.

Concerning the specific character of partisan political claims and promises, a Mid-Western paragrapher dryly observed that:

Probably the funniest thing that has developed in our national politics lately is the horrified fear of the residue of the Ohio Crowd lest Tammany get hold of the Government and corrupt it.

Probably it is. But the sense of fact and reality conveyed by this observation is not by way of disparagement of either the Ohio Crowd or Tammany, but of both together equally. The many-headed American sovereign at once gets the implication, by no means new to his consciousness, that political parties, whatever their conventional designation, really divide themselves only into the Ins and the Outs. The Ins are in and wish to stay in, while the Outs are out and wish to get in; and both the Ins and the Outs will cheerfully authorize any sacrifice whatever of collective or personal integrity, or both, to attain their ends. Another paragrapher conveys the same implication a little more delicately, thus:

Of course, we don't aim to be mean about it, but we can't help noticing that all this Mississippi water got loose under a Republican Administration.

Some of us are old enough to remember the hurricane of obloquy that came down on poor old General Hancock for saying that the tariff is a local issue. Here was a capital instance of a courtier invading the jester's bailiwick and encroaching on his privileges; for General Hancock was a candidate for the Presidency, and the many-headed sovereign was keeping close watch on his attitude towards the established conventions. The conventional, official, correct approach to the tariff was by way of showing that it was necessary only for the revenue, as the Democrats said, or, as the Republicans contended, for the protection of labor's right to work, or to keep the dinner-pail full, or to keep the blight of European pauper-labor competition off our infant industries. No one dared remotely hint that the tariff was a device for swindling the domestic consumer out of the difference between the competitive price and the price as augmented by the amount of the tariff-duty. No one, that is, except the Court Jester; he could make as free as he liked with this idea, and the sovereign and the boys would wink at one another, and have a jolly laugh all round. But General Hancock had no such privilege. His remark carried the most serious implications of lese-majesty, and it got him out of royal favor in no time at all.

If the question of the tariff is revived, as we see some prospect that it will be, a distinct set of conventions will be devised for the approach to it—the serious and official approach. Such are the traditions of absolutism. We cannot yet be sure what the conventional lines of approach will be, but we can be sure that any mention of the fundamental fact of pilferage committed upon the domestic consumer will remain outlawed from court etiquette. Any hint that the tariff is a mere delegation of the taxing power into the hands of court favorites—in effect exactly what the old royal method of tax-farming used to be—will put the offender into outer darkness, to keep company with the puzzled shade of General Hancock. The jester, however, while all this is going on, will regale and refresh his mighty sovereign with such observations as this:

Florida fruit-growers want a protective tariff now. Their democracy ends at oranges and bananas.

Or this:

Well, the French action on tariffs ought to call our attention again to the great truth that an infant industry thirteen feet tall looks peculiar in rompers.

Or the following comment on a tendency that we all perfectly well understand, but can by no manner of means seriously discuss:

What the French seem unable to understand about our elastic tariff is why it always stretches upwards.

The relations between the United States and England have long been the object of a very distinct court etiquette, and they may not be approached realistically, except at risk of the usual pains and penalties. We have all noticed this particularly in the reports of our various institutes and schools for the study of international affairs, as well as in the day-to-day editorial comment on our foreign policy. Realistic treatment of the late irruption of the Mayor of Chicago, for instance, is not permissible. To be strictly loyal to our sovereign's code, probably we should not even permit ourselves to think realistically about it; yet just that is what everyone does, the sovereign himself necessarily included. Hence the sovereign gets back a pleasing echo of his inmost thoughts from the paragrapher's observation that—

Big Bill Thompson says he is going to make a bonfire of all the books that have pro-British propaganda in them.

But how will he find them, unless maybe the bankers out there are easier than ours, and make a practice of letting the Mayor have access to their ledgers?

Well, the United States has immense power and an immense deal of money; and what Government situated as England's is, and with the Heaven-sent help of language-monopoly, would not strain every nerve to keep on the blind side of so much money and power? If there is not pro-British propaganda at practically every crossroads in the United States, then it would seem that the City and the British Foreign Office, with all their innumerable satellites in journalism and statecraft, stand convicted of sheer lunacy. Just so long as the United States has a lot of money and power, so long it will be infested with the vermin of British propaganda, French propaganda, Fascist propaganda, and every other kind that thinks it has any faint chance of drawing blood.

Far above and beyond court etiquette, there are of course always certain distinctions of taste involved in a creditor's attitude towards a debtor. Observance of these distinctions, however, is by no means inconsistent with reservations *in petto* which make up a vivid regret at having been misled into a bad investment; and this is what we discern in the paragrapher's mournful observation that—

Every day, in every way, Europe gets nearer and dearer to the United States.

—and also in his remark that—

Secretary Hoover advises caution in making loans to Europe. It is excellent advice, and only about $11,000,000,-000 late.

Perhaps the most rigid and sensitive conventions in our whole court etiquette are those that surround the American conception of success. America was always a land of opportunity in a double sense. It afforded a great opportunity for production, and hence a great demand for labor at a high wage. It also afforded a great opportunity to exploit production through certain forms of legalized monopoly, and through what we know under the euphemism of "financial operations." This latter form of opportunity was, obviously, not the one to be talked about; and the more the other form was glorified and kept to the front, the easier it was for the latter to escape undue attention. So we have always heard a great deal of the "gospel of work and thrift," and, naturally, those who had profited most by the exploitation of production were the most forward in promoting this doctrine; the most notable living example, no doubt, being Mr. John D. Rockefeller.

Circumstances have lately taken a good deal of emphasis off America as the land of opportunity for the rewards of work and thrift, though it is probably as much so at the moment as it ever was. But our court etiquette is still quite stringently against a realistic intellectual acceptance of certain notable American codes and practices as so many devices for the looting of production. Yet in regard to this, which I repeat is probably the most sensitive of our court conventions, the jester's privilege remains free, open, and acceptable to his squeamish sovereign. A paragrapher lately remarked that—

> As a result of the recent rise in the stock of the New York National Bank, George F. Baker is reputed to be $7,500,000 richer than he was ten days ago. This shows what hard work will do for a man.

Another extremely sensitive set of conventions are those surrounding our general organization of influence upon public opinion through advertising and press-agentry. It is so sensitive, indeed, and its authority is so far-reaching and effective, that anyone who makes the faintest motion towards a serious infringement upon it will instantly find every avenue of public expression closed to him. Yet even here the jester remains free to bring out the most subversive implications regarding these practices, as when he says:

> There are cigarettes now that will stop coughs, help the singing voice, and make one feel happy and contented, but we are not going to rest satisfied until some manufacturer puts one on the market that will stop hair from falling out.

Or again more subtly, as when he says:

> Our private opinion is that no one is really as competent as Herbert Hoover is supposed to be.

Not only is the jester freely privileged to bring out these implications against the objects sheltered by our conventions; he brings out implications that are still more subversive against the whole code of etiquette itself—one may say, against the convention of erecting a convention:

> The same kind of people who think a subsidy is merely a little subvention, and that imperialism is benevolent assimilation, think a lobbyist is a legislative superintendent.

The conventional line of approach to the question of disarmament and international peace leads through Geneva and the headquarters of the League of Nations. Loyal courtiers of the many-headed sovereign must keep up the fiction of following that line, and the more preposterous the fiction becomes, the more doggedly and mechanically they must stick to it. The jester is under no such necessity. A paragrapher lately set off the conventional view and the realistic view side by side in the same paragraph, thus:

> Commander Savage, of the American Legion, said in Paris: "It is a splendid sight to see Europe at peace." It isn't, but it would be.

Another paragrapher brings out the plain and natural but officially inadmissible truth of the situation, thus:

> Nations aren't likely to beat their swords into ploughshares while beating their rivals into oil-fields.

Still another sums up the recent discussions of disarmament in a similar vein of realism:

> The big idea is that it is a fine thing to have plenty of armament, so long as it is not being used in a warlike manner.

Similarly, the official and serious line of approach to the American Legion's recent junket in France is by way of Lafayette, the Unknown Soldier, and the great ideal of Liberty and Democracy. There are absolute considerations of taste and manners, quite apart from the arbitrary code of our court etiquette, which suggest circumspection in dealing with the idea that there was collaterally, at least, a more realistic motive behind France's spectacular hospitality towards the Legion. Nevertheless, that idea is not absent from the sovereign's mind, and he finds his own shrewd suspicions reflected from the coincidence brought to his attention thus:

> "Paris Delighted over Convention's Success," says one headline. "Legion spends $15,000,000," says another. And putting the two together . . .

III

If one were drawing the regular conclusion from all that has been set forth, it would perhaps be in the vein of fault-finding with the persistent human preference for pretense and make-believe over fact and truth, the persistent dislike and avoidance of realism. Yet the larger one's experience of men and things becomes, the more difficult and inappropriate this complaint seems. "What a Bedlamite is man!" said Thomas Jefferson in his old age, after years spent in observing this inveterate aversion to realism. There is no possible doubt of it. He also said, as others after him have said, how likely it is that the other planets use this one for a lunatic asylum. Yet he did not say these things despondingly, for, true as this view of our mundane affairs undoubtedly is, one cannot become indignant about it. In the present state of human development nothing else seems possible, or if it were possible—here is the great point—nothing else seems really very desirable.

One can conceive of a world of perfect consistency, a world governed absolutely by realism, that would be highly interesting to live in—much more interesting than our present world—if it were peopled exclusively by spirits like Thomas Jefferson. But unfortunately there is not enough of that kind of population available at present to go around in such a world; and, considering the kind of population that is available, such a world, if one could bring it into existence overnight, would be very dull. Think of a world governed by common sense, reason, and justice, but actually inhabited by human beings who had not yet outgrown the ordinary predilections that we know and see exhibited on every hand— who would wish to live in it? The old materialistic conception of Heaven, even, had to postulate an entire population of transformed and improved beings to inhabit it, for any other kind would have found it intolerable.

Considerations like these effectively check the rise of indignation in the radical devotee of reason and realism. They checked it in Thomas Jefferson, in Socrates, in Marcus Aurelius, in Jesus, in all who have had a wide experience of human affairs and made a proper use of their experience. These spirits took a large and lucid view of human inconsistency, never giving themselves over to it, but never on the other hand letting it overbear their reason and judgment, or derange their temper. Marcus Aurelius praised his predecessor, Antoninus Pius, as not having in him "anything, one may say, *carried to the sweating point*," and this was great praise. But as radicalism is commonly understood—and indeed as it commonly takes shape in the social bearing of its professors—one sees profound penetration in the paragrapher who lately remarked that—

The true radical is a man that thinks you are against him if you can't get as excited as he does.

But a man who has the sense of time as a factor in education, and the sense of the amount of development necessary to create a world governed by realism, or even to make oneself at home in such a world, cannot get excited. He quietly takes his stand with the king's jester, shares his realistic view, and does what can be done to further it by a method analogous to his. For it is the only method that is effective. One of our paragraphers says most profoundly that—

Another thing we have noticed in our journey through this old vale of tears, etc., is that anything that has to be protected from being laughed at, deserves to be.

Just so. We all know that our pretense is protective. Our diligent pretense about politics, statesmanship, the tariff, the

American standard of success, the League of Nations, and so on—all this, as in Hans Christian Andersen's fable of the king's new clothes, is a protective device to keep a laughable thing from being laughed at. But the method of crusading against pretense, arguing against it, inveighing against it, is relatively ineffectual. It is a method inevitably handicapped by the personality and temper of those who use it. On the other hand, men like our paragraphers, as has been well said, mightily help along the cause of truth "without encumbering it with themselves." Their method is impersonal, unevangelical, persuasive, and disarming; all their shrewdness, their radicalism, their experienced, realistic sense of the plain natural truth of things, find free play. They arouse no animosities, alarm no pride of opinion, nor do they seek to beat a person off his chosen ground—under their influence his ground imperceptibly changes with him. One must be aware that in respect of pretense and make-believe, as in other respects, human perfectibility has a long way to go. We may well believe it will go the full distance, and in that assurance we may well wish to help all we can in the process. The only question is, how best to do it; and here it would seem that the function of the king's jester and his modern counterpart affords a very profitable and interesting study in method.

ALAS, POOR YORICK!

An Apology for the Human Race

T HE MOST charming city on the Rhine—one of the most
charming in all Germany or in the whole wide world for that
matter—is the city of Bonn. Tourists usually manage to miss
it, and thereby miss a good deal, though their loss is Bonn's
eternal gain, probably; so in the general balance of things
one can afford to be philosophical about it. Yet it is strange
that Americans who have a sense of history and an eye for
quiet, cultivated, and rather opulent loveliness are not oftener
attracted to Bonn; especially since it happens to have (with
one exception—the Straubinger, at Gastein) the most pleasant and beautifully situated hotel that I have ever seen in a
long lifetime of pilgrimage from one hotel to another. Touring is a hard business, and when one has done just about so
much of it there is clear profit to the spirit in dropping off
at Bonn for three or four days, to rest and think it all over—
maybe to wonder whether a maximum of mileage in a minimum of time is really a dividend-paying proposition. Three
days in Bonn is sure to breed doubt of it. One feels the steady,
slow tempo of German life, the life that has plenty of time
for everything. It has plenty of time even for living; you perceive this as you stroll along the beautiful river-promenade
on a late summer afternoon or evening, and you also perceive
how the art of living is practiced—you get a technical lesson

in this fine art if you keep your eyes open, and it makes you wonder whether it may not be an art worth cultivating.

As you sit on the hotel terrace you have a superb river view, or panorama, from the Seven Mountains down to the handsome bridge that carries a vivid reminiscence of Julius Cæsar. This enterprising marauder improvised a pretty good bridge at almost the exact point from which the present bridge springs. The Germans, with a vast respect for this achievement, have put up a fine bust of Julius at the bridge entrance, with a Latin inscription stating that he was the first person to bridge the Rhine. It brought back to my mind an idea I have had for twenty years—that some technical expert with imagination and a turn for good writing could make an interesting book about Cæsar's engineers. To a layman, the engineering problems involved in his campaigns, from end to end, seem to show that he must have had some experts on his payroll in the engineering line, whoever they were. I should like to see those problems dissected from a professional point of view and expounded in a popular style that I could understand.

The whole region of the Rhine's left bank is replete with antiquities of Frankish and Roman times, and earlier. Bonn has its share. The Provincial Museum contains no end of relics of the Roman occupation. Among other interesting items, an attendant showed me a counterfeiter's outfit for the manufacture of bogus Roman coins, remarking sagely that even the Romans had their *Spitzbuben*. I was immensely interested in the vast number of luxury-products in the Museum: jewelry, fancy combs and hairpins, mirrors, perfume-bottles, vanity-boxes—go through the whole modern apparatus of personal adornment, and you would hardly turn up an item that was not there in counterpart. It was the old story of good commercial enterprise; trade following the flag. The moment the legions had the region pacified the rascally Roman go-getter swarmed in to corrupt the natives with his trumpery; no doubt he had all the latest wrinkles on how to "break down sales-resistance." As a good American, with proper pride in the ideals of Mr. Ford and Mr. Hoover, I duly mustered up a few tears to shed on this unknown pioneer's grave if I could find it; but no one seemed able to tell me where it was.

His works, however, live after him, and he has contemporary mention from one who knew him well and knew all the ins and outs of his pitiful little game—Julius Cæsar. Years ago, when the Germans invaded Belgium, all our newspapers, I believe, carried Julius's estimate of the Belgians in standing type. "Of all the Gallic tribes, the bravest are the Belgians." Well, that was all right as far as it went, but I was amused to notice that nobody ever cited the reasons that Julius gives for the Belgians' ability to keep up this fine spirit. He gives three. The first one is that the Belgians are farthest removed from the Roman Province and the apparatus of its civilization! The second is even more striking, "because salesmen very seldom get through to them with a line of goods that tend to weaken the character." To a person who knows what wars are for and how they start, there was a vast unconscious humor in our quoting Cæsar's praise of the Belgians. A tourist going through the Rhineland with Baedeker in one hand and Cæsar's Commentaries in the other, will learn a great deal about the whys and wherefores of war, and thus save himself the wear and tear of getting worked up over the nostrums proposed for abolishing it.

II

The museum at Bonn contains the skull and a few bones of the oldest inhabitant. This veteran is known as the Neanderthal Man, and he is quite a celebrity in his way, being one of the earliest known specimens of our human race. He was discovered at Neanderthal, a village not far from Bonn, in the course of some commercial excavation, I believe; and savants have calculated his probable age by the estimated aggregate age of the geological formations which covered his remains. There is a chart in the museum that shows just how all this was worked out. The savants have also "reconstructed" him in plaster of Paris by conjecture, according to the hints given them by his bones. If their efforts are to be trusted, he was no great beauty, apparently, judged by our present standards, though to a professional eye like the late Mr. Tex Rickard's, for instance, he probably had points. His skull was shallow; he was a low-brow. His legs were short, his body long in proportion, and his arms very long. His eyes were uncommonly deep-set, and his lower jaw protruded like a bulldog's, whereby his countenance took on a sinister expression that would have marked him out even among Chicago's best assorted. All in all, one would say he was probably bad medicine, and if one met him *redivivus* in the middle of the road one would not argue with him about the right of way.

Nevertheless, I got a great deal of highly valuable "orientation" as I believe the logothetes call it, out of looking at him. I do not know how many years ago he lived. I did not notice what the estimates were, nor have I since boned up on any of his vital statistics. I only noticed that he was one of the two or three earliest known samples of my race, and the one succeeding thought interested me so much that it promptly extinguished any curiosity about figures. The thought was this: that my race—the race of man—has been on earth so short a time that I can still look at a few fragile survivals of one of the earliest. A frail human skull, a trifle of lime molded up by nature's processes into a highly perishable shape, has outlasted the whole development of civilization up to date.

Probably no one can make a very sound guess at the age of the world. A scientific gathering was discussing it in New

York a few weeks ago, and their conclusions summed up to something like this: that this earth, for every year it had existed since animal life appeared on it, had existed nearly a thousand years before animal life appeared. This throws animal life relatively late. Then, relatively much later in the course of animal life, man suddenly appeared. Expressed in figures, the earth is perhaps nine hundred million years old; animal life has been on it for perhaps nearly a million years; and man has graced the scene for some thirty or forty thousand years, possibly. But aside from figures, the fact is that the Neanderthal Man lived so short a time ago that his frail bones are still here and still in such shape as to give us a pretty good idea of what he looked like and of his grade of development towards what we should call nowadays a civilized being.

III

One might say, I suppose, that civilization may be roughly measured by the distance—not in time, but in culture—between this lowly brother and ourselves. The sight of his remains suggested very forcibly to me that civilization has really done fairly well to get as far along as it has got, considering the relatively brief time that has elapsed since it started. Some of us are dissatisfied with our civilization, complain about it, and are discouraged by it. I have done my share of all three. The first two are quite all right; our civilization is certainly a poor enough affair, anyone who is even half satisfied with it ought to be ashamed of himself, and everybody ought to kick about it as hard as he can, poke fun at it, ridicule and satirize its shabbiness, meanness, childishness, and spiritual poverty. Especially should everyone throw mud and bricks at the disgusting airs it puts on when it goes on dress-parade. There cannot be too much of this sort of thing done. When there is any let-up in the steady exercise of hard-boiled self-appraisal it is a sign that the progress of civilization has stopped for the moment, and that something had better be done to start it up again. But to be discouraged, sullen, or sour over the situation is another matter; it indicates that one is expecting more of civilization than it can possibly give him—which is impracticable. All of us are strongly tempted towards that frame of mind, I think, at one time or another (I know I am), and the best specific that I have discovered against this temptation is an hour's spiritual communion with the vestiges of the Neanderthal Man.

There cannot be too much social criticism or too many critics. We cannot have too many Upton Sinclairs, Menckens, Villards, Lewises. For every one we have, we could easily do with a dozen. I am all for frying Babbitt over a slow fire; and I would joyfully pillory all the Rotarians and all the energumens of Service from Duluth to Baton Rouge. When Mr. Villard digs up the tomahawk and goes after some rascally politician's scalp, I rejoice; also when he kerosenes the Daughters of the American Revolution, and applies a match. The more "Middletowns" are picked on to be surveyed, and the more thoroughly they are surveyed, the better I am pleased. When Mr. James Truslow Adams trains his guns on *Fordismus*, Hooverism, and the theory and implications of mass-production, I would be proud to tote ammunition for him. But a social critic ought to have some training in the perspective of his job; and if I had my way, I should round up all these earnest and disinterested promoters of our spiritual welfare, convoy them to Bonn, and give them about two weeks of monastic life in the Provincial Museum, in prayerful contemplation of the remains of our poor departed relative.

It is the world's best preparation for the exercise of social criticism, for, when all is said, the essential, the really significant difference between the first-class and second-class critic

—or let us rather say, between the effective and the less effective critic—is in a temper, a frame of mind. Figuratively speaking, Swift and Juvenal never trued up their critical spirit by the spectacle of the Neanderthal Man, while Socrates, Rabelais, and Cervantes did. Socrates knew the Athenian politicians really a little better than Mr. Villard knows those of Washington, because he measured them instinctively by Athenian society's general relative distance from the Neanderthal Man. He knew that they were mountebanks and scoundrels, and that Athens was in for a bump, but he also knew that nothing could be done about it for another twenty or thirty thousand years, because Athenian society at large was simply not up to the point of doing anything or wishing anything done. Hence he did not behave like another Jeremiah or Solomon Eagle, crying "Woe to this wicked city!" He did not denounce the political situation, or—as a current word alone expresses it—bellyache about it. He simply drew a picture of the situation, colored it with exquisite unruffled humor, and hung it up to stay as long as the world lasts. Rabelais sized up sixteenth century Babbittry-plus-ecclesiasticism about as completely as Mr. Lewis and Mr. Mencken have sized up the Baptist-Methodist-Elk-Rotarian Babbittry of our land and time; and some little Babbitts there were, loose in France in his period. But he was aware that human development had got just about that far, so he took a good picture of it at that stage, and left it as a permanent exhibit. He was raised in the country, and knew there was no sense in raging around an apple tree in August because the apples were green, when they could not possibly be ripe before September. Since the Neanderthal Man's frail skull has not disintegrated yet, it is a good deal to suppose that his leading characteristics, good and bad, can have been very largely washed out of his offspring.

IV

This prehistoric brother used tools and, such as they were, he depended on them mightily. His mind, what there was of it, was highly practical, as much so as Mr. Ford's or Mr. Hoover's. It was centered on his tools and on what tools would do, and he knew that the better his tools were, the more and better they would do. He was not a reflective person; his intellect did not habitually range beyond the immediate purpose of his tool-using. He had what we now call the short-time point of view. Results—immediate results—were what counted with him; and when his mind focussed on the immediate thing it did so with all its strength.

The other day I passed through that marvel of engineering skill, the New York Central yards, on an outbound train. I remember well when the new station was built at Forty-Second Street, and how the building was completed and the yards rearranged without error or accident and without stopping a single train. Traffic went on as usual. Such a performance in tool-using was probably never seen in the world. I amused myself with thinking, as I always do when I go over that intricate trackage, how an adult human society will estimate that achievement several thousand years hence, assuming that a complete record of it will somehow be available. I venture to say that the man of the future will marvel at it as sincerely as we do, and that he will then proceed to laugh his ribs loose, as any reflective person must do to-day, at its inconsequence. What is it for? To help get people, say, from New York to Chicago; that is, to transport them from the kind of life one lives in New York into the kind of life one lives in Chicago. Also, to help transport materials in order to sustain the kind of life one lives in both places. It will strike the man of the future as the oddest and most laughable thing in the world that here were people with intelligence enough to create this marvellous mechanism of transportation, intelligence enough to operate it, but without intelligence enough to create a better collective social life for themselves than the life lived at either end of this railway system.

The man of the future will laugh at this, but he will understand it. The fact is, probably, that the power and habit of reflection have developed down from our old relative in Neanderthal in a pretty fair ratio to our development in tool-using. One cannot expect much better. Life in New York and Chicago is first-rate as a matter of mechanics; it is satisfactory to anyone who is chiefly a tool-user—which is what most of us are. The immense mechanism of railways, banks, finance companies, factories, export trade, automobiles —the Neanderthal Man would look all this over with great approval, once he got used to it, and he would say that his progeny had done very well by themselves. The fact of its being devoid of other satisfactions would not trouble him especially. He would not be in the least impressed at hearing that Plato, Virgil, Dante, or Rabelais had voted the life of Chicago and New York utterly odious. Well, then, why should those to whom he bequeathed the immense preponderance of the tool-using power over the reflective power be more impressed?

The Neanderthal Man, again, had a turn for being predatory. He took what he wanted when he could get it, and the idea that he was taking it away from someone else—if indeed it ever occurred to him—caused him no pangs. He was out for himself; his number was number one. If he were abroad in the world to-day he would soon feel quite at home among the devices that his progeny has invented for the same purpose. He would be charmed, for instance, with the superiority of a tariff over his old-fashioned knotted club, and of poison gas over his hand-to-hand war weapons. He would see whole nations, as well as individuals, acting pretty regularly as he used to do, and he would have no trouble about

recognizing the great predominance of the instinct for spolia-
tion that he left as one of his special legacies. He would see
this instinct organized with a thoroughness that he never
dreamed of, and large bodies of men planning and conniving
day and night to make it effective. In all this he would see
the working of the short-time point of view, and he would
like that, because it was his own. The long-time point of
view, largely established by the history of past events, meant
little to him. In his estimation, "history is bunk"; it throws
no valuable light on the future. In short, our old friend would
be quite in his element in contemplating the aims and ideals of
our industry, commerce, and politics.

V

Alas, poor Yorick!—we know him well. It will take the
race a long time to breed out the little characteristics that he
ingrained into it. A good many generations of "practical
minds," morons, captains of industry, financiers, opportun-
ists, and robots must come and go before that takes place. It
might seem that all the machinery we have developed might
aid humanity's higher qualities to make a better showing than
they do; but these qualities have not yet had time even to
make a start. Ever since the old days in Neanderthal man has
been a creature of action and invention and, only very lately
and very fitfully, a creature of thought and reflection. Even
now he thinks only as the force of circumstances drives him
to it; he does not enjoy thinking and never does it when he
can get out of it, even to his own loss and damage. He will
be a long time developing his reflective powers up to the
point of interesting him in their exercise as much as he is interested in exercising his powers of action and invention.
What do the educatonal ups and downs of a few thousand
years amount to in a line of development that is reckoned in
hundreds of millions? All Western Civilization, the civiliza-

tion of action and invention, informed by a glorified predatory Neanderthalism, could go by the board overnight without furnishing even a colorful incident in a march of events
laid out on such an august scale.

Nor is this a depressing reflection. The sight of our de-
funct kinsman should not put on us the wet blanket of an
inert fatalism. It only shows us clearly what we may and may
not expect. It connects our criticism properly with both the
past and the future, and thus insures its balance of judgment.
It keeps us from the short-time point of view in criticism,
from an unduly close preoccupation with the present. Mark
Twain was one of the ablest second-rate critics of society,
and it was only the Neanderthal bent towards the short-time
point of view that kept him from being a first-rate critic.
There is a strong flavor of Neanderthal in the maxims of
Pudd'n-head Wilson, in Mark Twain's fits of rage against
"the damned human race," and in his project for exterminat-
ing the whole breed by withdrawing the oxygen from the
atmosphere for two minutes. Perhaps, too, one can see the
short-time point of view, an imperfect connection with the
future, in the critical efforts of Mr. Villard, Mr. Lewis, and
Mr. Mencken. The bulk of the first-rate critic's business is
with the future; he sets a mark for the race to grow up to,
using the present only as a point of departure. That is what
Socrates, Rabelais, and Cervantes did; and because they did
it their works are still with us.

After all, our sturdy old friend at Neanderthal did about
the best he could, and if one gets at him right, he may have
been to a certain degree suggestible. He was no doubt wary
and suspicious, but it is not inconceivable that he could have
been worried into some sort of momentary and fitful intro-
spection by the wise, calm, playful, urbane, tolerant, disci-
plined superiority of the first-rate critic. He might, and very
probably would, have subsequently treated the critic much
as his spiritual progeny treated Socrates, but, nevertheless,

one can imagine that he had his moments of self-examination. Something like this is the only service that the first-rate critic can hope to render the present, and in serving the future it thus sometimes happens that casually, occasionally, and without premeditation, he serves the present too.

For Babbitt, the hierophants of Service, the Baptist-Methodist-Elk-Rotarian denizens of the Bible Belt, are also doing about the best they can, and so are Mr. Ford and Mr. Hoover with their salvationist doctrine of mass-production. The future will have its own opinion about them, and the first-rate critic's business is to anticipate the future, work with it, and look exclusively to it for his dividends. Nevertheless, out of all these there may be some who are not wholly inaccessible to the suggestion that their best is pretty poor and that it might be better. So, quite incidentally, the first-rate critic, through the tone and temper which the very absence of preoccupation with the present gives his work, may do his own time, as well as the future, a useful service.

While, therefore, as I said, I am always exhilarated by our contemporary critics' lively mode of attack, I am always conscious that it is the Neanderthal survival in me which responds to it, and that such a mode really serves neither the future nor the present. I would wager that the French politicians were much more uneasy when Anatole France was around than when they were listening to the diatribes of the reddest Communist in the Chamber. The Communist was for the moment only, but they knew that Anatole would last a long time and that his sapping and mining of the ground they stood on would increase in efficiency with the passage of generations. Meanwhile his easy and imperturbable superiority probably nagged some of them, at least, into a self-conscious sense of their own spiritual poverty. I doubt whether Mr. Villard moves his Neanderthal statemongers to self-examination, or Mr. Mencken his Neanderthal sectarians. I doubt whether Babbitt ever suspects that Mr. Lewis has the future on his side, for indeed Mr. Lewis's tone would seem to show that he himself is none too certain of it.

Alas, poor Yorick!—his leading traits are doomed to extinction, and he never got very far with the traits that are appointed to supplant them. Only lately has the race begun to have a glimmering of how interesting the newer traits are, and to suspect that they are worth cultivation; only lately has humanity made any room for them. It is advantageous to realize just how much we are justified in expecting from so recent a development. Touring parties are all the go just now, and so I suggest one, somewhat in the nature of a pilgrimage, for the dissatisfied, discouraged, disbelieving, for the vigorous, second-rate social critic, for those obsessed with the present and its shortcomings, for the perfectionist advocate of this-or-that social nostrum warranted to cure overnight. I suggest that they charter steamships and, as soon as the fine weather comes on, repair to Bonn.

IF ONLY—

I

CONSIDERING THE untold tons of garbage that are shot daily from our presses, it would be an intrepid person who should demand a new book on any subject. Nay, with books no longer the symbol of light and leading that they once were, but now become only a symbol of *was uns alle bändigt, das Gemeine*, no one with a literary conscience would ever so faintly suggest that another should be added to the list. Some years ago, I asked one of our ablest publishers how he got books out of his authors. He said, "I don't. On the contrary, I do everything in my power to keep them from writing books." I have always treasured the memory of this publisher and honored him as a loyal friend, not only to literature, but also to me; for while I, poor sinner, have fallen from grace once or twice since then, his words have kept my lapses at a minimum.

How many of us wretched addicts, indeed, should such words put in the way of giving literature the very best service we could possibly render! One thinks of Thiers's profound remark to Count Walewski, who, not content with a career in diplomacy, vainly imagined he could write a good play. "What possessed you to do it, Count?" said Thiers, on the first night. "It is so hard to write a play in five acts; and it is so easy not to write a play in five acts." How can temptation rear its head against this solid wisdom? Yet it does. At

the present moment, for example, now that this idea has occurred to me, I am tempted to make it the subject of a long
essay, in the hope of touching the flinty hearts of publishers,
editors, literary agents, and above all, the deceitful and desperately wicked people who organize literary competitions.
But I forbear; though the impulse is almost overpowering, I
shall resist it, for in the cause of righteousness one good example is worth a thousand precepts.

Again, things being as they are, one's literary conscience
would not only stay one from suggesting a new book, but
would also admonish one to go very gingerly about recommending a new book to the attention of any public, large or
small, general or special. With the noisy vogue of bad taste
and vulgarity everywhere rampant, the public is deafened to
every voice that is not pitched in the shrill falsetto of utter
self-abandonment, and hence the sober appraisal of a new
book may easily be taken as its proverbial damning with faint
praise. Then, too, even in recommending a serious book to a
very small and special public, as I have twice lately ventured
to do, one is uncomfortably conscious of Emerson's sound
principle of never reading any book, no matter what, that is
not at least a year old. Of contemporary literature, indeed,
even serious literature, one can hardly read too little—*man
lese nicht die mitstrebende, mitwirkende*, said Goethe—and
almost invariably the mere passage of time discloses any contemporary critical estimate of it as worthless.

But though one may not ask for a new book or even recommend one, I suppose one is still free to say what sort of
new book one would most enjoy reading. I imagine one might
permit oneself to do this, provided it were done on the clear
understanding that one had nothing in view beyond the in-
dulgence of a harmless whim. I hope so, at any rate, for I
have long had such a book in mind, and now, having made
manifest the spotless purity of my intentions, I should like to
say something about it.

II

It would give me a deal of pleasure to read a historical essay that followed out two lines of speculation, one of which I am quite sure has never been explored at all, and the other only a little way. History is notoriously a chapter of accidents, and historians have often entertained themselves by speculating on the probable changes in the course of events if this-or-that accident had not happened precisely when and as it did. If, for example, an unknown soldier's bullet had not pierced the breast of James Wolfe, on the Plains of Abraham, would George Washington ever have been the leader of a successful revolution? If Napoleon had not been laid up with a bad cold in the head, would he have shown better strategy at Borodino, demolished the Russian army, and turned the campaign of 1812 into a brilliant success which might have altered the whole course of subsequent European history? Speculation on accidents of this order is common enough. There are, however, two extremely commonplace types of accident which I believe have never been properly considered in their historical aspect; that is to say, I have never seen more than a bare hint of any speculations concerning the probable course that history would have taken if in certain given instances such accidents had not intervened.

Hence I should be delighted to read an essay which considered, first, the accident of individual poverty from the historical point of view. Twenty-five or thirty years ago I applied myself to a long study of the works of Henry George, which led me in turn to look closely into the circumstances of his public career and private life, and into the fortunes of what is commonly known as the 'single-tax movement,' which was launched into American politics towards the turn of the last century. I wondered then, and have wondered ever since, whether George would have consented to put himself and his philosophy at the service of an Adullamite political jehad if he had not been always so miserably poor. It seems most unlikely. His instinct was strongly against doing anything of the kind, and the cast of his mind was so eminently philosophic that one might expect him to have regarded the politics of America as Socrates regarded the politics of Athens—as something, that is, for a really sound politician to keep as far as possible away from. Instead, however, of concentrating his energies on remaining a man of thought, he divided them, and became in great part a man of action. One might make out a good case for the thesis that the corrosive action of poverty inflamed a naturally ardent and nobly sympathetic temperament to the point of making him peculiarly accessible to the urgings of what Mr. H. G. Wells calls the Gawdsaker—to the point where immediate action, even ill-considered action, in behalf of those as poor as himself seemed a paramount duty.

This being so, it is interesting to speculate upon the historical position that George and his economic philosophy might even now occupy if the determining factor of poverty had not been present. Indeed, a thoughtful person might find that the principal effect of a close survey of this remarkable man's public career is to make one wonder what his influence would amount to at the present time if he had not been so poor.

Similarly an essayist might find a first-rate exercise for his imagination in trying to estimate the force of Napoleon's dire poverty as a factor in the fate of Europe. In all that has been written about Napoleon I doubt that this has been done. Even *War and Peace*, which sets the high mark probably forever as a masterly job of deflating and debunking a historical personage, leaves this factor out of account; yet it must have been considerable. Napoleon, as Count Tolstoy says, makes his first appearance in French history as "a man of no convictions, no habits, no traditions, no name, not even a Frenchman"; moreover, he was dead broke, unsuccessful and despondent, an adventurer, offering his sword here and there, with no takers. The irregularities of his conduct in the French service caused him to be struck off the list of general officers, September 15, 1795; he was in disgrace. Nevertheless, the most extraordinary freaks of chance—a deadlock of partisan political forces, the puerile incompetence of his colleagues, the insignificance of his opponents—opened the way for a free exercise of "his frenzy of self-adoration, his insolence in crime and his frankness in mendacity," whereby his career was made.

Now no doubt these opportunities lay open to any adventurer who happened to find himself on the spot at the moment, and if one had not been there, another might, and the consequences to Europe might have been quite the same. Napoleon certainly had no monopoly of the very moderate amount of sagacity that was needed to perceive the prospect which these freaks of chance held out, and to profit by them. But that is not the point. The point is whether, for example, if his father, dying in 1785, had left him a good substantial income, Napoleon would have been on the spot when the moment came, or anywhere near it. One may reasonably doubt that he would. It is highly probable, almost certain, that the moment would have found him much more congenially employed elsewhere, very likely at home in Corsica; his previous history gives a distinct color to this supposition. I imagine that if he had chosen to stick to the practical side of military affairs, as seems most likely, he would have ended his days as a first-class competent artillery officer, high in the service; and if he had gone in for the theoretical side, he might have made himself another Clausewitz or Moltke. I believe that a disinterested examination of the matter would show that the basic reason why the disgraced Corsican adventurer, Nabulione Buonaparte, found himself on that particular spot at that particular moment was that practically all his adult life he had been poor and busted and looking for a job. Very probably, too, it was the sudden reaction from this condition that enhanced all the evil qualities in his nature and made them dominant, for this is what so regularly happens in such circumstances that its regularity has given rise to the common proverb concerning the risks of putting a beggar on horseback.

The essayist might have even more fun out of examining the career of Louis-Napoléon in the light of this idea. An anonymous writer of the last century says he knew Louis-Napoléon well for twenty-five years, and was almost certain that if he had not been so poor as he was, there would have been no Second Empire. A great deal can be said for this view. Even granting that he would go back to France in 1848 and put himself up for the presidency of Lamartine's ramshackle Second Republic, one might find pretty good ground for believing that as a rich man he would have been content to stay in that position and do what he could with it, rather than incur the risks and animosities involved in disintegrating republican solidarity and honeycombing the Legislative Assembly of 1849, in preparation for a *coup d'Etat*. But the more one considers the state of French politics ensuing upon the fall of the July monarchy, the less reason one sees why, if Louis-Napoléon had not been poor as Job's turkey, he would have dreamed of going back to France at all.

I shall not anticipate the essayist by recounting the conditions, subjective and circumstantial, which make this seem probable. Suffice it to say that but for his hamstringing impecuniosity, Louis-Napoléon was doing extremely well where he was. Always a studious and reflective man, in spirit much more a philosopher and poet than an emperor, he might have lived on very pleasurably in London, developing his ideas on free trade in association with Richard Cobden and John Bright, and in correspondence with Enfantin, the Périers and Michel Chevalier. He might have written his projected history of Cæsar, continued his studies on the abolition of poverty, and no doubt made quite an impressive thing of his twin schemes for an international currency and for what would seem to be a very practicable sort of United States of Europe, based on the suppression of customs frontiers. English society had received him most favorably, putting its best resources at his disposal for the beguilement of his lighter moments; while for those still lighter, he had the devotion of the blonde Miss Howard, who appears to have made herself always entertaining and delightful—and there is some evidence that her rôle in the drama of his life in London carried several capable understudies as well. As far as one can see, the only "out" in this excellent situation was his distressing poverty.

I believe one could draw up a highly plausible argument for the thesis that but for this one factor there would have been no Second Empire, and hence doubtless no calamitous messing about in Italian, Mexican and Oriental affairs; probably a satisfactory composition with Prince von Bismarck in the middle 'sixties, such as almost any bourgeois republic, however imbecile and venal, but alive to its own interest, might easily have arranged; indeed, Louis-Napoléon himself had two capital chances to arrange one, and flubbed them both. Above all, there would have been no Mlle. de Montijo, and hence no Wissembourg, Wörth, Spicheren, Sedan; and for the probable changes ensuing in English, German and Italian history, a whole volume of speculation would hardly be enough. As it stands, that history was determined by a skillfully pumped-up revival of the "Napoleonic tradition," and the primary spring of action behind that revival may well have been Louis-Napoléon's poverty. The various stories about his unshakable faith in his "star" have very much the air of something put out after the fact; or, as the sinful would say, the air of being mostly hooey.

The anonymous author whom I mentioned a moment ago

says that after witnessing two days of the revolution of 1848 he never read a word about any of the revolutionary movements that took place in France during the nineteenth century. It was enough for him, he says, to know that these movements were invariably led by men in want of five or ten thousand a year. My essayist might look into this matter a little; my notion is that he would find plenty to reward him. It was the accepted understanding among those who were "in the know" that Lamartine proclaimed the Second Republic for money. The great orator was at that time not only in his usual state of being flat broke, but also about $70,000 in the red, and hounded by creditors. With a republican revolution under way, and a right smart chance of himself being president of the republic, he could get his debts paid; as in fact he did. He was somewhat a Daniel Webster of his time; and it is not unreasonable to suspect that his financial disabilities may have had a great deal to do with making him the fugleman of the shouts for a revolutionary republic.

The essayist might make similarly interesting finds among men who were prominent in the other upheavals that France went through after 1789. He could probably turn up something out of the White Terror of 1815, a good deal out of 1830—Louis-Philippe never let himself or anyone else forget how desperately poor he had been; his preoccupation amounted almost to a mania—more out of 1851, and he could fill a long chapter with a study of the needy political adventurers of 1870-1873, Gambetta, Favre, Jules Simon, and their fellow-strivers. While on this last period, too, he might digress for a moment to note a striking example of the effect of individual wealth upon the course of history. When the National Assembly met at Bordeaux in February 1871, it is almost a certainty that if the Orléans family had bestirred themselves in their own behalf, their dynasty would have been restored; which means that if this family had not been rich enough to keep out of the unwholesome prairie-dog's nest of French politics at that period, there would have been no Third Republic.

I have cited this century of French history only because it affords so many conspicuous and consecutive examples of the kind of thing I mean, and not at all implying that my essayist could not find plenty elsewhere, for they are like the sands of the sea for multitude wherever politics exist. Plenty such he could find in our own history, without rattling any skeletons in our neighbors' closets. I have in mind one statesman who influenced the course of our political history most profoundly, whom beyond doubt poverty nudged into politics in the first instance, as the easiest way to keep his body and soul together. I would give his name, but that his memory is dear to many, and some of them might think I was going out of my way to disparage him.

III

My mention of Mlle. de Montijo, better known as the Empress Eugénie, appropriately introduces my essayist to his second line of research, which is a study of henpecking from the historical point of view. All of us who have maintained even the most formal and austere relations with the fair sex may be presumed to have a fairly clear theoretical idea of what henpecking is; some of us, unhappily, perhaps most of us, have got our knowledge of it at the hands of that harshest of pedagogues, experience. My dictionary defines henpecking as domineering by one's wife; but when one thinks of Mme. du Barry and Mme. de Montespan, when one thinks of grandmothers, mothers-in-law, maiden aunts, elder sisters and *Gott soll hüten* débutante daughters, this seems a very limited definition. One might put it more generally, I think, that henpecking is the habitual imposing of the female's will upon the male, whereby the male's disposition towards the matter at issue is overridden, and his will nullified.

The strategical methods employed in this exercise are very various, running all the way from the hawklike possessiveness of Mme. Polosov, the tragic tears of Mme. Karenin and the freezing hauteur of Lady Dedlock, to the intransigence of Mrs. Raddle, the bickering of Mrs. Caudle and the strong-arm methods of Mrs. Proudie. Those who know more of such matters than I do tell me that by nature practically every woman has all these methods at immediate command, and is also gifted with an extremely fine tactical sense in the matter of their mobilization and deployment. I suppose I might add that my own desultory observations rather tend to bear out this view.

The anonymous friend of Louis-Napoléon, whom I mentioned a moment ago, says in the course of some observations on the Empress that no one has traced the effects of henpecking on the course of history, and he cites some instances in support of his statement. Nevertheless he is not quite right. The henpecked man has mostly been fair game for the Jerrolds and Gavarnis of the world, but the essayist and historian have also sometimes taken him quite seriously. One's real complaint is that they have not followed through on him, not given the factor of henpecking anywhere near all it is worth, not as a rule taken more than its immediate consequences into account; whereas its more remote consequences are often the most important. For example, in the cardinal instance of Jeanne Poisson's henpecking Louis XV into the Seven Years' War, they do not go beyond the immediate political consequences to France, usually stopping with the defeat at Rossbach, the loss of Canada and the extinction of French influence in India; whereas the really interesting thing about this bit of henpecking is what it did to Germany and the German spirit, and what might have befallen these if the lady's seductions had not worked.

Maria-Theresa, wishing to recover Silesia, got together a group of nations in an alliance against Frederick the Great. To make this alliance strong enough, she had to get France into it; so she sent that strange creature, Prince von Kaunitz —albeit a first-class diplomat, though one hardly sees how he could be—over to Paris to labor with Louis XV. France had just come out of the war of the Austrian Succession with about as much to show for it as the United States got out of the war of 1914, and Louis felt towards this new proposal somewhat as Senator Johnson might feel towards a suggestion from the French Government that we should go over to Europe in force this summer and help exterminate Hitler. Von Kaunitz encountered a deaf ear and a marble heart; there was nothing doing; so he took the matter up with Louis's lady-friend, Jeanne Poisson d'Étioles, Marquise de Pompadour, and got results. It seems that old Frederick, who was nothing of a lady's man, regarded Jeanne's pretensions with blunt Prussian derision, and had lampooned her outrageously in some pretty salty verse—he could do that sort of thing rather well when he felt like it—and Jeanne looked upon Maria-Theresa's project as a providential chance to get even.

This was the prelude to the Seven Years' War, which left Prussia flat; it was only Elizabeth of Russia's death in 1762, and the immediate withdrawal of Peter III from the alliance, which enabled Frederick to win the war by the skin of his teeth. This victory, coupled with those of the two preceding wars, no doubt laid the foundation for the Germany of 1870-1914; but the preceding wars had also firmly consolidated the German spirit, the superb *Ernst der ins Ganze geht* which the domestic policies of Frederick and his father had liberated and fostered, and which was to make the later Germany the most highly civilized nation of Europe. As far as this consolidation was concerned, the Seven Years' War was superfluous and useless; and as far as the development of those policies was concerned, it was mischievous and retarding, for all the power and resource of the German *Geist,* which might have been so fruitfully employed otherwise, had to be concentrated on the problem of sheer physical recovery from the terrible blows which had well-nigh scourged Prussia off the face of the earth.

If, then, Jeanne Poisson had not henpecked Louis XV, Frederick would have had seven clear years of comparatively easy going in the administration of Prussia's internal affairs; and the question at once arises, what would have been the effect of those years on the future of Germany, not only as a factor in international politics, but also, and of far more consequence, as a moral and intellectual force in the world? Even under the handicap of the Seven Years' War, that force, as we all know, has been very great; and the fact of its having been so great adds interest to the conjecture at what it might have been, and might now be, but for that handicap.

The line of investigation in this instance is fairly easy to follow. For one that is less so, if the essayist cared to go back as far as the year 1535, he might look into the political consequences of the henpecking of Ercole, duke of Ferrara, by three of the most unbearable Frenchwomen who ever gained a place in recorded history. Then there was Prince Menshikov's Lithuanian servant-girl who seems to have put Peter the Great up to most of the good things he did, and also some bad ones, and who habitually burned the ground around his imperial moccasins when he did not show enough alacrity about heeding her suggestions. She became Catherine I of Russia, and if Catherine II's polyandry had not preëmpted the interest of our prurient reading public, she would no doubt be quite a figure in our modern fictional biography. Again, there was Sophia-Dorothea, whose henpecking of her husband resulted in the death of her first-born son, which opened the way to the throne of Prussia for her second son, who is known in history as Frederick the Great. Again, there was

Susanna Wesley, who, despite her absorbing labors as the mother of nineteen children, still found time to hold the bullwhip relentlessly over her husband and her son John, who became the founder of Wesleyan Methodism. So one might go on through a long and varied list, from the contemplation of which one arises with an enhanced respect, perhaps tempered by some little touch of uneasiness and apprehension, for the astounding qualities of generalship therein set forth and made manifest.

IV

"Why, of course that is true," cried a vivacious French friend, with whom I lately broached this topic of henpecking. "Who does the milking in Europe? The women. The American woman won't do it, so the man must, with the result that presently he is bored with it, and invents a machine to do it for him. She won't sweep; the man gets tired of living in squalor, and rather than do the sweeping himself, he invents the vacuum cleaner. She won't cook; so for a while the man risks dyspepsia and ptomaine poisoning on the utterly uninteresting food which your public eating places provide, and then invents automatic toasters, roasters, boilers, fryers and God knows what-not, on the forlorn chance that he can get something out of them that is fit for a dog to eat. She can't think, can't read anything worth reading, can't converse intelligently, can't sit still; the man puts up with her restlessness as long as he can, and then invents the automobile, the radio, the motion picture, in order to take her out of herself, and thereby give him a few hours of peace.

"If you looked into it, I believe you would find that henpecking is responsible for half the so-called labor-saving gadgets in the world; and I assure you, my friend, this henpecking has made considerable history already, and is making more every day. It goes against my grain to say so, for I

like your people and admire the many good things they have
done, but I believe they are fast taking leave of their ancient
and inbred integrities, and are setting up instead the ideal of
a national life which shall yield all good things to everybody
at the touch of a button. My understanding is that you call it
the More Abundant Life. I call it a life without any worthy
purpose to guide it, without intelligence, without principle,
without conscience—in a word, without character. I don't
like many things that are going on at home in my own country, and still less do I like some things that our neighbors are
doing; but neither they nor we are setting up any such ideal
of a national life as that. Your Mr. Hopkins said as much last
fall in an issue of that magazine which you sometimes write
for, and he is right. More of you ought to be saying the same
thing, and saying it straight from the shoulder, for if you per-
sist in following after that ideal, you may take it from me
that it will sink your civilization straight down to Peg Trant-
tum's, as our old friend Panurge says, fifteen fathom below
the corridor that leads to the black pit of Demigorgon."

My friend's imagination may have been a little over-
wrought, though I do not imagine he meant to hold the influence of our women wholly responsible for this unpromising
state of things; yet no doubt their influence must be reckoned with in casting up the sum of that responsibility. But
we are not concerned with this at present, for I cite the conversation only as suggesting still another point of departure
for a research which the essayist might find rewarding; and
with that I bring my little flight of fancy to an end. I reiter-
ate my belief that poverty and henpecking have never been
appraised at anything like their actual importance in determining the course of history; and while, as I said at the outset, I would not dream of asking for a book on the subject
or take the responsibility of recommending one, yet if such a
book should by any chance appear, it would be just the book
that I should like to read.

EPSTEAN'S LAW

A FEW DAYS after Mr. Willkie's nomination I happened to see a published statement from him in which he flatly accused Mr. Roosevelt of promoting the idea of Statism; that is to say, the idea that the individual exists for the State. He said that he himself believed the exact opposite of this; he believed that the State exists for the individual. Mr. Willkie added that this issue—the issue of individualism *versus* Statism —was the issue on which he intended to make his campaign.

I do not know whether or not Mr. Willkie has carried out this intention or even said anything more about it; but that is my own fault because, what with one thing and another, I have not got around to following the course of the campaign. His statement attracted my attention, however, because it fell in with a line of thought which I was then pursuing in consequence of having read certain recent books. Last spring several authors came out with essays proposing various practical policies, all of which were based on the idea which Mr. Willkie accuses Mr. Roosevelt of promoting. It struck me then that if any of these policies were to be proved workable, it would have to pass three tests; tests which are so simple and commonplace that anybody can apply them, but which, because they are so simple and commonplace, hardly anyone ever thinks of applying, although —when all comes to all—they are the tests by which every general political policy must stand or fall in the long run. Now, if Mr. Willkie means what he said and is elected, he will presumably formulate some sort of general political policy or line of procedure to implement his idea that the State exists for the individual. On the other hand, if Mr. Roosevelt is elected, he will no doubt even more energetically continue the policy implementing his idea that the individual exists for the State. My purpose in writing is to show that all the reader need do to convince himself that either policy is workable or unworkable is to apply to it, if and when it is announced, the three tests I shall now go on to indicate, using some of last spring's crop of political essays by way of illustration.

I

I might begin with a story. When I was a very young man someone showed me a sheet of manuscript music which was a curiosity in its way. It was written for the cornet. I read it over and saw that it was very good music indeed. The trouble was that no one could play it, because the composer had neglected to put in any rests where the cornetist could take breath. This omission made the whole thing utterly impracticable. It seems to be in the order of nature (at least as far as we at present understand the order of nature) that man cannot push wind in a cornet continuously for any great length of time; he has to stop and refill his lungs every once in a while. This incapacity may be a misfortune for music or it may not; but, in either case, there it is and apparently nothing can be done about it. Therefore what this composer was actually trying to do was to introduce disorder into nature by building his music upon a putative human capacity which does not exist. He made a failure of it; and the point is that a moment's reflection on the nature of man not only would have shown him that failure was inevitable, but also would have shown him plainly why it was inevitable.

One of the books which came my way last spring was Mr. Max Eastman's *Stalin's Russia and the Crisis in Social-*

ism. It brought the foregoing story to my mind at once. Mr. Eastman says he was for twenty-five years a Marxian socialist, accepting the Marxian policy for organizing human society according to the formula, *From each according to his abilities, to each according to his needs.* On this he remarks the curious fact that it never occurred to Marx to ask himself just what there is in human nature to give him any assurance that society can operate on that principle. Furthermore, Mr. Eastman says, for ninety years Marxian socialists have been assuming that a simple State collectivization of property would lead directly to the establishment of such a society as Marx contemplated. On this Mr. Eastman remarks as an odd fact that during those ninety years "not one Marxian has ever raised the simple question: Is human nature, as it has developed in the struggle for survival, sufficiently self-dependent and sufficiently coöperative—or sufficiently capable of self-dependence and malleable in a coöperative direction—so that a collectivization of property would actually lead to the society of the free and equal, the dying away of State power, the condition of felicity described in the formula, 'From each according to his abilities, to each according to his needs'?"

Well, rather! One would indeed suppose that it might have occurred to somebody to raise this question, especially in view of the fact which Mr. Eastman points out, that the work of Darwin, Huxley, Herbert Spencer, and a whole shoal of other investigators into the nature of man and the conditions essential to the maintenance of human society, all took place during those ninety years. Marx and Engels wrote the Communist Manifesto in 1847, and *Social Statics,* Spencer's great exposition of the fundamentals of social organization, appeared in 1851. Surely at some time within the century it should have occurred to any literate Marxian to ask himself what he has found in the intellectual and moral capacities of mankind to give him any ground whatever for believing that the Marxian formula is practicable. The question is obviously fundamental, for what is the use of getting up a fine attractive prospectus for the organization of society if the realizing of it turns out to be repugnant to the order of nature, and therefore will not work? Marx, as Mr. Eastman shows, was precisely like the composer whose music could not be played because it did not take proper account of the inflexible order of nature.

Mr. Eastman, like all good doctrinaire Marxians, was somewhat taken aback at seeing how quickly, easily, and apparently naturally the Marxian system in Russia slid off into an autocratic régime of outrageous tyranny. He now thinks some modification of the Marxian prospectus is necessary. His proposal is to organize "a new scientific radical party" which "to begin with shall marshal the proletarian class-forces behind some such programme as that which Max Lerner calls 'democratic collectivism,' envisaging a society in which 'private property and private industrial initiative would remain; but the capitalists could make their decisions on policy only within a framework set by planning-boards.' It would assert, as Lerner does, that a democratic capitalist society *can* plan, 'if the majority and its leaders have the courage to take capitalism away from the capitalists, and make its basic decisions socially rational and responsible.' "

Just so; but once bitten, twice shy. Once more the obvious question is, what have Mr. Eastman and Mr. Max Lerner discovered in the constitution of human nature, the mental and moral make-up of mankind, to assure them that society can operate to any better purpose on the principle of "democratic collectivism" than on the principle of Marxian collectivism? It may be conceded to Mr. Lerner that "the majority and its leaders" have plenty of courage to take away from anybody anything which is not spiked down. He need have no anxiety about that. But just what is it in human nature

which warrants the assumption that when "the majority and
its leaders" have taken capitalism away from the capitalists
they will make their basic decisions any more "socially rational and responsible" than the capitalists have made theirs?

Again, Mr. Lerner's system is fundamentally Statist; it
contemplates an area of voluntary coöperation only within
a ring of State-enforced coöperation. Mr. Eastman ac-
cepts it as such. His proposal is (italics mine) that "we
must surrender to coöperation *and the attending State
control* as much of our individual freedom as is indispen-
sably necessary to the operation of a complicated wealth-
producing machinery." In his view, however, there must
be some sort of guarantee that the measure of State
control shall not become excessive. We must proceed,
Mr. Eastman says (italics mine), "in search of guarantees
against the totalitarianism *which now seems inherent in State
ownership.*" In another place also he postulates "a scheme of
distribution for an economy of abundance *not* involving
totalitarianism," and says that after surrendering so much
of our freedom as may be indicated for the success of the
scheme "we must guard with eternal vigilance the rest." All
this is unquestionably very fine, very good, but just what
is it in the constitution of man which gives Mr. Eastman the
idea that anything of the sort is practicable, or that after his
democratic society has made the initial surrender it will not
continue gravitating steadily towards the *Führerprinzip?*
With his own actual experience of democratic societies in
mind, just what does Mr. Eastman find in the physical capacities of man to make him think that his scheme, or Mr.
Lerner's scheme, would not pretty promptly run up into
what Mr. J. P. Mayer so well calls "a plebiscitary dictatorship"? Moreover, what does he find to support the notion
that this régime of dictatorship would be *ipso facto* less
totalitarian, less oppressive, corrupt, spendthrift and generally
vicious, than any other?

On Mr. Eastman's own showing, it appears to me that this is the first test to which any political proposal should be subjected. If it had been applied to Mr. Roosevelt's general policy in the first instance we might have been spared considerable misfortune. If Mr. Lerner's interesting variant of Statism passes this test, or Mr. Eastman's, well and good; if not, they are out of discussion. Mr. H. G. Wells has drawn up a whole imposing Magna Carta as a basis for the organization of a peaceful and prosperous world-society; Mr. John Chamberlain advocates what he calls with unconscious humor "a mixed economy"; while others among their co-Statists offer various suggestions in less detail. All these should be put to the same preliminary test—can the moral and intellectual capacities of mankind stand the strain of supporting them when put in practice? Can they, as we say, "take it"? If so, then let us consider them; if not, then not. Let us freely admit that Marx and all his Statist progeny have composed superb good music, wonderfully attractive and fascinating when you read the score, but if it can't be played, and if ordinary common sense is all one needs to see clearly why it can't be played, then what is the use of saying any more about it?

II

So much, then, for the first test of this or that politico-economic general policy: Is there anything in the observable order of nature which can be counted on to give it active support? Now for the second test: Is there anything in that order which can be counted on as actively against it? And here again I should like to illustrate what I have to say by recounting a bit of personal experience.

For a long time I have held to a politico-economic doctrine which has been before the public for many years. As it appears on paper it is so nearly perfect that nothing worth listening to has ever been said against it, or can be said. It is simple as the Golden Rule, and as far above criticism. It is as competent as the legislation of the legendary king Pausole who had only two laws on his statute-book, the first being "Hurt no man," and the second, "Then do as you please." If I were legislating for a society of just men made perfect, I should set up my doctrine at once as a practical scheme, exactly as it stands. Things being as they are, however, I do not advocate it or expound it or try to convert anyone to it. When acquaintances occasionally ask me about it I refer them to certain books, and let it go at that. This rather lackadaisical attitude is due to the fact that long ago I applied to it the two tests which I am now expounding, and got a negative result. I could find no principle in human nature favorable to my scheme, and I did find one that is dead against it. This principle is the one set forth in the fundamental law of economics, that *man tends always to satisfy his needs and desires with the least possible exertion.*

Man-at-large appears to follow this principle in common with the rest of the animal world, and to accept its guidance as implicitly as any cow or cat in the land. In fact, my philosophical mentor Edward Epstean puts it down, I think quite correctly, as the second law of nature, rating self-preservation as the first; so for convenience we may call it Epstean's law, even though Mr. Epstean was not the first to formulate it. Like the first law, it admits of occasional short-time exceptions. Considerations such as ambition, prudence, fear, pride, decorum, sometimes come in on occasion to make man act against this principle, but he always *tends* to act in accordance with it; and experience abundantly shows that he does so act with a regularity and persistence which are far more than enough to make hay of my politico-economic doctrine. My doctrine simply will not work, and as long as Epstean's law remains in force it can never work. Let us see how this is so.

There are two means and only two whereby man can satisfy his needs and desires. He can do it by work; or he can do it by appropriating the product of other people's work without compensation. The second means obviously involves less exertion than the first; therefore man, acting under the operation of Epstean's law, always tends to employ it. When he can employ it legally, moreover, common observation attests that he invariably does employ it. The legality of his action, of course, rests with the State; it is the State which gives him the privilege of employing this means without risk of being had up for it and put in jail. A profitable land-grant, for example, conferred by the State, has often legally enabled persons to satisfy their needs and desires with no exertion whatever. A tariff levied by the State enabled the late Andrew Carnegie and his associates legally to appropriate without compensation a vast deal of wealth produced by other people's work, and thereby to satisfy their own needs and desires most prodigally with little or no exertion. Hence, in view of the profitable possibilities resident in State action, man is always under the heavy pressure of Epstean's law to induce the State to take action in his behalf.

The State, however, must be administered, and the only administrators available are folks, people, human beings; and human beings in administrative positions are quite as amenable to the operation of Epstean's law as they are elsewhere; if not, as a rule, more so. It requires far less exertion, obviously, to sit in the House or the Senate or on some administrative commission and direct the distribution of other people's wealth to one's own advantage, than it requires, say, to cultivate corn in Illinois or whack steers in Texas, and thereby produce wealth for oneself. Hence, as long as the State stands as a potential distributor of economic advantage, Epstean's law works powerfully and harmoniously in and out between those who seek that advantage and those who can confer it. The consequence is that on the one hand the

State tends progressively to multiply its functions as an auctioneer, while on the other hand the administrative field tends to become a sheer stamping-ground of professional adventurers. It is observable also that the wider this field is opened, as in the self-styled "democratic countries," the more freely and largely do these tendencies come into play. For example, I believe that never in the world was there so stupendous a demonstration of the force of Epstean's law as is furnished by the growth of Washington's population in the last eight years.

All this stands to reason as natural and inevitable. The more functions the State takes on, the further its range of control is extended—in short, the closer its approach to a totalitarian character—the more of other people's wealth becomes available for its administrators to appropriate and dispose of as they see fit; and consequently the larger will be the number of their political adherents and dependents. Hence the greater will be the attraction for cynical adventurers with a gift for making the most of these circumstances; hence also the progressive exclusion of any but cynical adventurers from the field of politics—and those, moreover, of a progressively lower and lower order. The most casual glance at political history in any period since the great irruption of *soi-disant* democracy first broke upon the western world is enough to show that this is so; and also to show that the untoward consequences which we are now witnessing have come about in strict conformity with the incidence of Epstean's law.

The faculty of instinctively applying the same order of disinterested and objective criticism to one's own philosophical system that one applies to a competing system is extremely rare. This faculty is one of the marks which distinguish a critic of the very first order; it distinguishes an Erasmus or a Rabelais from a Calvin or a Luther. A Unitarian theologian, for instance, may be, and usually is, a first-rate critic of Trinitarian theology, but a very lame critic of his own theology. Similarly Mr. Wells, Mr. Eastman, Mr. Lerner, and our philosophers of the New Deal, all make a fair fist at criticizing what they call the capitalist system, but do not seem aware that the same order of criticism which they apply to it is also applicable to their own several variants of State collectivism. As we have seen, When Mr. Eastman criticizes doctrinaire Marxism he seems vaguely aware of the existence of Epstean's law, for he speaks of "the totalitarianism which now seems inherent in State ownership," but when he broaches Mr. Lerner's variant of State collectivism as a substitute doctrine, he seems never to have heard of it.

So when he and those who are like-minded come forward with proposals for surrendering some of our individual freedom "to coöperation and the attending State control," the judicious reader will call a halt until this phrase can be mulled over and cleared a little. Any degree of economic control carries with it a corresponding power to distribute economic advantage; in fact, it *is* that power. A power of control which does not carry this power of distribution is unthinkable; any talk of it is simply a contradiction in terms. Clearly, then, "the attending State control" at once opens the way for Epstean's law to become operative. Hence Mr. Eastman should be asked how he would prevent its operation from going on indefinitely to the confiscation of further liberties. He might reply that "we must guard with eternal vigilance" the unsurrendered remainder, but *quis custodiet custodes?* The reader will remind Mr. Eastman that *all* of us alike—both the guardians and those, if any, who guard the guardians—*all* tend to satisfy our needs and desires with the least possible exertion; and therefore the assumption that this tendency would not pretty promptly prevail over any purely hortatory incitement to vigilance seems extremely shaky. Again, if Mr. Eastman produces the scheme which he appears to think producible, "a scheme of distribution for an economy of abundance *not* involving totalitarianism," the judicious reader will ask just what derailing device, if any, Mr. Eastman has in mind which can be counted on to switch off the operation of Epstean's law at any given point short of totalitarianism.

III

The tests which I have been discussing hang on the moral and intellectual capacities of mankind. The third test hangs on mankind's affectional capacities. A full discussion of these matters would probably be a rather delicate business, so I shall say only enough about them to make my point clear. It seems to be in the order of nature that man's affectional interests have but a short radius of action. They do not normally reach much beyond one's immediate family or a small entourage of intimates, if indeed so far. Philanthropy (using the word in its strict etymological sense) usually contemplates an abstraction; possibly even Abou ben Adhem, if he had disinterestedly overhauled his own affectional capacities and taken their exact measure, might have found it so.

This disability, if it be one, cannot safely be presumed upon in constructing a politico-economic policy. The danger is a double one. If a policy is designed to stretch man's affectional capacities much farther than they will normally go, it sets up a damaging revulsion, and in the end breaks down. More than this, it powerfully reënforces the operation of Epstean's law in bringing about odious political abuses, all the more odious because they are brought about under the ægis of enlightened philanthropy.

Summing up now, whatever policies or practical proposals may be made by Mr. Willkie or Mr. Roosevelt, or indeed by anyone, the judicious reader will do well to apply to them the three tests which I have set forth. First, is anything discoverable in the moral and intellectual capacities of mankind which will support them? Second, do they run aground on Epstean's law? Third, do they tend to stretch the affectional capacities of mankind beyond the limit which the order of nature appears to have put upon them? Many social philosophers have tried to construct systems which would jump these three hurdles, and have failed; chiefly because, as Mr. Eastman shows, they did not know the hurdles were there. Probably the thing could be done—I think it might be—but whether it can be done now and here is another question, things being as they are. At all events it is useful to be aware that, as long as our socio-political architects do not know what the hurdles are and where they are, it will not be done.

SUNDAY IN BRUSSELS

To Munson Havens

My Dear Friend:

You are a charming correspondent, fully entitled to a leather medal, because you never ask any fool questions. You have never even asked me what I think about the international situation and the chance of war, which is Fool Question No. 1. Just for that, I am now going to uncork all the inside information which I have been picking up at great expense in the various European chancelleries these last six months, and much good may it do you.

You probably remember the story of the sea-captain who told a fussy old woman that the best time of year for her to cross the North Atlantic was when she had the money and wanted to go. There you have my best guess on the chance of war. There is a chance of war whenever someone wants to grab something and thinks he can get away with it. That is the international situation at the moment, exactly as it has always been ever since nations existed. The chance of war is precisely what it was when the planet was first infested by what old Frederick called "this damned human race," *diese verdammte Rasse*. A hundred and fifty years ago Chief Justice Jay said that "nations in general will go to war whenever there is a prospect of getting something by it"; and that is all any Foreign Office can tell you now, or could ever tell you.

It is not very definite information, maybe, but it is all

186

there is, and there isn't any more. How do I know, how does anyone know, when somebody is going to gamble on a net gain out of starting a dust-up, or who that somebody will be? But while I can't say much that is definite about the international situation or the chance of war, I can say a whole lot that is definite about the International Situation and the Chance Of War, and I shall be pleased to do so. You may take the tip straight from the horse's mouth that the Chance Of War is the Big Out nowadays, and the International Situation is that infernal scoundrels are working it to the limit everywhere in Europe, just as they are in the United States, according to what I read and hear.

Governments (which is to say, being interpreted, job-holders) are looting, terrorizing and brutalizing whole populations without let or hindrance, all on the Chance Of War. They are perpetrating the vilest swineries against human rights, liberties and decencies, all on the Chance Of War. Everywhere here the Chance Of War is tightening the grip of Nietzsche's "coldest of cold monsters, the State" on the individual's neck. The Chance Of War covers every device that a despicable ingenuity can invent for reducing human beings to the loathsome condition of State-servitude. The Chance Of War justifies every means of breaking the human spirit, mechanizing conscience, prostituting ideals, and debauching conduct to the level of savagery.

You see I am describing the International Situation objectively and in a general way. I should like to give you three or four volumes of my opinion about it, but I thought you would probably rather have the unvarnished facts. If you were here I don't believe the thought of war would cross your mind once a week—it doesn't mine—because you would see so much going on that is worse than war. I always thought the old-line pacifists were barking up the wrong tree when they laid so much stress on the horrors of war. I confess I can't get up any tootle about slaughter, pillaging, bombing, stinking people to death with gas, and all that sort of muck, though I have been closer to a goodish bit of it than I care to be again. To my notion, the real horror of war is what happens to people when the war is over, and the greatest horror is when the Chance Of War begins to get in its work. I was in Europe during the last war, and most of the time since, and for a choice of horrors give me war every time.

Mr. Jefferson said that the spirit and manners of a people are what really counts, and so they are. They are pretty nearly all that counts, and their destruction is the real horror of war. Think of the incredible degeneration which set in on our people after the last war, and ran on through the twenty-year period which was such a fine curtain-raiser for the revolting mess we are now in. It was not peculiar to us; it hit us harder, but one can see its boils, blains and pestiferous botches sticking out everywhere here in Europe also. In a word, that war took twenty years out of the life of every civilized person in the world, and no one knows how much more it will take before it gets through.

Compare those twenty years with four years of actual war, and the sum-total of bombings and shootings seems pretty middling trivial. True, you and I are alive and the bombed fellows are dead, so as a matter of sheer animal instinct we might put ourselves down on the lucky side, but how about it, really? Pyrrhus was right, ἄβιος βίος, βίος ἀβίωτος, which we might construe as meaning that a sickly spiritual life is just no life at all. If you and I had not accumulated enough spiritual capital out of the older culture to see us through, albeit in an exiguous and rather lonesome fashion, should we not have been glad to call it a day twenty years ago? I think so; and how many people who have dragged through these twenty years have had our advantages? Precious few. Besides, what right has any contemporary civilization to make a person live on his capital instead of chipping it into the general cultural pot to help produce and distribute a bigger general fund of spiritual wealth?

Seeing what goes on, I sometimes think that, as a principle of political organization, nationalism is pretty well on its last legs. It is a fairly new doctrine, running back only to the beginning of the sixteenth century, when there were but four national organizations in Europe, and rather loose ones, at that. Its fuller development has taken place within the last twenty-five years, following the breakup of the three great non-national empires into the national Succession States. Hence you might say it has been an experiment, so far, and like the experiments with artificial diamonds, or getting gold out of sea-water, the thing does not seem "commercially practicable." It costs too darn much. The overhead eats up all the profits, and the business will either have to be given up or go bust.

Look at the cost of National Defense, which politicians insist is necessary on account of the Chance Of War. Look at the prodigious cost of "social legislation" and all the other rapidly-mounting costs of maintaining nationalism. They must all come out of production, and there is no longer enough production to pay them and keep itself going. That is the trouble in every country where jobholders can make their people believe that the sacred ark of nationalism is in danger. They are facing the homely facts of fundamental economics which cannot be dodged or bulldozed. National organization is a great principle, if you don't weaken. It is all very fine and grand and puts up a wonderful show on dress-parade, but if you have nothing left to go on with after the bills come in, where are you?

When I was in England lately, I saw how remarkably successful the British jobholders have been in putting the wind up their people about the Chance Of War, and in consequence, how they are rifling their people's pockets with both hands. An English merchant told me (not by way of complaint, I hasten to say) that by careful calculation he was working nine months a year for his king and three months for himself. Of course I made no comment on this, but I could not help thinking that the mediæval feudal lord would probably not have pried much more out of him. It appears also that his king is going to raise the ante on him a little, for I was told that, what with five billion dollars' worth of National Defense and all, maintaining the principle of nationalism in England would come to something like twenty-five billion dollars next year.

Without exception, however, every Englishman I talked with told me that on a hard pinch the country might stand the national taxation, but the local taxation is the thing that is killing it. Two of them got out their tax bills and showed me figures which took my breath away. This was news to me. It seems that the local boards and councils are infested by uplifters and social-service zealots who are bung-full of schemes for succoring the downtrodden with schools, doles, pensions, free lunches, shorter hours, housing, playgrounds and the devil only knows what-all of other devices for running up the general overhead on nationalism. They are doing so well with these that when I left England the impression on my mind was that national defense and "social security" between them are cross-lifting the country's prospects into the Promised Land.

The worst thing old Bismarck did for the world, and he did a plenty, was to launch the idea that the State is a proper agency for social welfare. He was in trouble with his Socialists, so to take the wind out of their sails he cribbed the main items out of their "social security" programme, and worked them himself as a State enterprise. He had only an electioneering interest in the thing; it was merely a matter of putting off the evil day, like throwing out caps and boots to wolves. Later on, in the face of powerful Laborite agitation egged on by feather-brained and windy reformers, the British State thought to lengthen its lease of life by the same means; and I don't imagine you need to be told anything about what the American State has done and is doing in that line, or why it does it.

The idea, however, is now so deeply rooted almost everywhere that nothing short of an appalling calamity could kill it; yet see how preposterous it is. The State is no proper agency for social welfare, and never will be, for exactly the same reason that an ivory paper-knife is nothing to shave with. The interests of society and of the State do not coincide, and any pretense that they can be made to coincide is sheer nonsense. Society gets on best when people are most happy and contented, which they are when freest to do as they please and what they please; hence society's interest is in having as little government as possible, and in keeping it as decentralized as possible. The State, on the other hand, is administered by jobholders; hence its interest is in having as much government as possible, and in keeping it as highly centralized as possible. It is hard to imagine two sets of interests more directly opposed than these.

This opposition of interest is what fully accounts for Paine's excellent observation that "the trade of governing has always been monopolized by the most ignorant and most rascally individuals of mankind." Society has a primary interest in social welfare. The State has not; its primary interest is the interest of jobholders; and therefore nothing could be, worse done than what it undertakes to do for social welfare. Politicians leap with joy on this-or-that proposed advance in "social legislation," not out of any primary interest in social welfare, but because it means more government, more jobs, more patronage, more diversions of public money to their own use and behoof; and what but a flagrant disservice to society can accrue from that?

If you think these are only my own disordered notions,

let me tell you they are not. Not one of them is mine. I am taking them straight from Benjamin Franklin, so if you have any comment to make you should see Ben about it. But why care whose notions they are; why not put them to the test of experience? Let me tell you what to do. Blow the dust off your copy of Ben's *Autobiography* and turn to his observations on the reading of history, written May 19, 1731. There is only half a page of them. Make a large copy, frame it and hang it up where you can see it while you are reading your morning paper of any day when Congress or any other *turba atque colluvio* of politicians is in the news. That's all—except that it will be a handy thing to point to when some enthusiast comes along to get you interested in some new piece of "social legislation." You won't have to say a word; just call his attention to it and walk out.

The thing I can't make out, however, is what this great new dispensation is supposed to lead to, aside from what it does for politicians. I see how the More Abundant Life is a good talking-point for jobholders, but what else, exactly, is it supposed to be? Does it mean a rise in the general average of happiness? If so, that is a laudable object, for all the authorities from Saint Augustine down to Bentham agree that the attainment of happiness is the end and aim of human existence. Some say, though, that the More Abundant Life does not mean this. When Camille Mauclair was here in Brussels last winter, he reported a conversation he had been having with a reformer, which touched on this point. "Am I to understand," he asked, "that your idea is to make everybody happy?" The agitator replied, "Not at all. What we intend to do is to make the happy people unhappy."

If this be in fact the idea of the More Abundant Life, one must say it seems to be succeeding admirably, for the erstwhile happy people give every evidence of being none too happy now. The contrast here, for example, is striking. Thirty years ago, when Brussels was Brussels, there was no central heating to speak of, no gadgets, bathtubs were scarce and plumbing mostly didn't work, and people made their own amusements; there were no movies, radios, motor-cars, cheap excursions. Moreover, the whole social scheme was dead wrong. As Mr. Dooley's anarchist friend said, th' government was in th' hands iv th' mon-nopolists, and they were cr-rushin' th' life out iv th' prolotoorios. Perversely, though, the people as a whole were the gayest I had ever seen, and if the underprivileged and exploited prolotoorios themselves were not happy, they were certainly putting up a first-class imitation of it.

To-day I don't see anybody putting up any imitation at all. The mon-nopolists look unhappy, as probably they are, —M. Mauclair's friend has no doubt been attending to that, —but the prolotoorios also look unhappy, notwithstanding thirty years of effort to usher them into the More Abundant Life. All the gadgets in Christendom are here now; two huge department-stores are full of them. Socialism has long been top dog in the government, and pledges to hoist the suffering prolotoorios out of the Slough of Despond have been a commonplace of every election in thirty years. The people have more useless leisure and every sort of deteriorating commercial amusement to fill it; movie-houses abound, and while radios do not abound, neither are they scarce. Nevertheless no one, be he mon-nopolist or be he prolotoorio, looks or acts or sounds as happy as in the bad old times.

So all I can make out of the situation is that the general average of happiness has gone down a peg or two; but I may be wrong, at that. Perhaps the people are like the Irishman's wriggling snake, which he said was dead, "but he isn't sinsible iv it yet." Perhaps they are brimming with happiness, but have set up a fashion of imitating the English, who are said to take all their joys sadly. I somehow doubt this, but it is possible, of course. At all events the contrast between appearances now and appearances thirty years ago is distinctly appreciable, and appearances are all I have to go by.

I am in a bad frame of mind here. It fairly puts my dander up to see Belgium swamped under a steady stream of pauper refugees from Germany; not all of them Jews either, y' understand, not by a good many. These poor souls, after being maltreated and robbed of all they have, somehow make their way across the border with nothing in their hands but their lives, and this country is at its wits' end to know what to do with them. To close the frontier against them seems inhuman, for after all, they have "done got to be somewhere." They can't very well be driven into the North Sea, or treated like tramps or sturdy beggars. Belgium has always had a great tradition of liberty, and the people respect it and are proud of it. As you know, this is chiefly what has made Belgium the most attractive dwelling-place in the world for a person of my type of mind. So far, I believe, the government has done nothing to stop the influx of refugees, and the people certainly do not want it to do anything, but the situation is fast becoming so acute that the authorities will have to take some sort of action, however reluctantly, as Holland, which has the same tradition, has already done.

It strikes me that this is an outrage which is everybody's business wherever German refugees seek shelter, and I think my countrymen ought to take on their share of the business, and get properly hot about it. Don't misunderstand me. I would be the very last to encourage the great American lust for messing in on another country's domestic policies. But this is not a matter of domestic policy. Germany's policy may be what it may be, but when it litters up the whole face of the earth with paupers it is no longer a domestic policy. It is foreign policy of a most provocative character, and the nations that are embarrassed by it—of whom ours is one— are pretty tame cats, in my opinion, if they stand for it.

I observe that when we Americans get into one of our

hot fits against the German government's treatment of its undesirables we are most properly twitted with having done the same thing ourselves. So we did. When our revolutionary party came into power, it had on its hands a similar problem and took a similar course with it. We robbed and maltreated the loyalists, and harried them out of the country. We lost by it, too, for by and large they were the best people we had.

Quite so; but there was this important difference: we did not make ourselves a nuisance to the neighbors. I don't for a moment imagine we would have cared if we had, any more than the National Socialists care now; but as a matter of fact, we did not. Our refugees had a hard time of it, most of them, but they put no strain on any other country's hospitality or resources, as the German refugees are doing everywhere. Here is a perfectly valid ground of blistering resentment against the National Socialists, and I wish our citizens would take note of it.

Our old friend Frank Warrin tries hard to make me believe that America is ripe and ready for another Voltaire or Rabelais. It isn't. There would have to be about five centuries of intensive spade-work put in on American intelligence before either of those two worthies could do a dollar's worth of business in America. I do think, though, that another Socrates might come handy, and I know that at least he could have a world of fun in our glorious republic until the Senate Investigating Committee clapped him in quod.

Socrates knew nothing, and was proud of it. He carried the magnificent art of Not-Knowing to the legal limit, and oh, my dear friend, what an incomparably great and splendid art that is! He never formulated or organized anything, not even a science of semantics, and was also proud of that. Apparently he never wrote anything, unless the few fragments of playful verse which have come down to us under his name are really his. He did nothing but hunt out people who were cracked up to know a tremendous lot, and ask them questions about their specialties. When they used terms like Democracy, Justice, Planned Economy, Liberty, Individualism, Republican Institutions and so on, he would scratch his head and say naïvely that he wasn't quite sure what those meant; he hadn't it quite straight in his mind; he would have to have some more information about it. Then with one guileless question after another he would let the wind out of the wise man's wisdom until he had him looking like a deflated soap-bubble.

What a man for our time! How he would make hay of our politicians, economists, sociologists, and above all, our journalist-publicists! I have three of these last particularly in mind at the moment, whose papal tone is most exasperating —how one would rejoice to see a Socrates blandly chasing them up the chimney and out the top! I fear, though, that having got their science so neatly formulated, the semantickers will lose no time about organizing it, and then, good-bye to the chance of a Socrates.

Good-bye to you also, dear friend, for the time being. Write me when the mood is on. Nothing is minutiæ to me which you write or think.

ALBERT